Memory 101
for Educators

With love and gratitude, I dedicate this book to
Phillip "Thabu" Eloff, the South African member of our family,
whose influence and knowledge inspired the story of Opooit and Nyack;
the rest of my family—Scott, Josh, Amy, Marnie,
Madison, Max, Lucy, and Rigby;
the newest member of our family, Jackson Joseph Sprenger;
and in loving memory of Joseph E. Sprenger,
whose love and kindness are still an inspiration
to us all, and who left us with only wonderful memories.

Memory 101
for Educators

Marilee Sprenger

CORWIN PRESS
A SAGE Publications Company
Thousand Oaks, California

For information:

Corwin Press
A Sage Publications Company
2455 Teller Road
Thousand Oaks, California 91320
www.corwinpress.com

Sage Publications Ltd.
1 Oliver's Yard
55 City Road
London EC1Y 1SP
United Kingdom

Sage Publications India Pvt. Ltd.
B-42, Panchsheel Enclave
Post Box 4109
New Delhi 110 017 India

Printed in the United States of America

Library of Congress Cataloging-in-Publication Data

Sprenger, Marilee, 1949-
Memory 101 for educators/Marilee Sprenger.
    p. cm.
Includes bibliographical references and index.
ISBN 1–4129–2772–2 (cloth)—ISBN 1–4129–2773–0 (pbk.)
   1. Memory. 2. Learning. 3. Mnemonics. I. Title.
LB1063.S67 2007
370.15′22—dc22   2006001790

This book is printed on acid-free paper.

06   07   08   09   10   9   8   7   6   5   4   3   2   1

Acquisitions Editor:	Faye Zucker
Editorial Assistant:	Gem Rabanera
Production Editor:	Beth A. Bernstein
Copy Editor:	Brenda Weight
Typesetter:	C&M Digitals (P) Ltd.
Proofreader:	Dennis Webb
Indexer:	Sylvia Coates
Cover Designers:	Lisa Miller
	Scott Van Atta

CONTENTS

PREFACE

A STORY WITHIN A STORY

I have been teaching classes on learning and memory for many years. Participants have included people from all walks of life who are worried about their own memories, or how to help a loved one. Many are educators who want to know more about how memory works, how they can help themselves, and especially how they can help their students. Questions they have include:

- Why do my students forget things from one day to the next?
- Why do my students forget information we have reviewed for the test?
- Why do I forget where I put my keys?
- Why do I forget where I parked the car in the parking lot?
- Why do I forget a name twenty seconds after I'm introduced to someone?
- Why do I forget appointments?
- I have to learn something new for my job; why do I keep forgetting?

I found it interesting that they focused on what they were forgetting. It brought to mind the saying that "elephants never forget." With that thought, I decided to create a tale explaining this phenomenon. So, the lion king Nyack, which is a South African word for "strong hearted," and Opooit, which means Old Foot, the name of a legendary elephant of South Africa, were born. Researching these great animals was enlightening. Elephants are very bright and have no natural enemies besides humans. They *do* have extraordinary memories. The African lion has been considered king of the jungle due to size and strength. Like the elephant, lions only have humans to fear.

Using memory strategies and suggestions from memory research that I teach in my classes, the acronym N.E.V.E.R. F.O.R.G.E.T. developed. To assist my class participants, I then added a mnemonic device, a memory trick, to further establish in their memories what each letter of the acronym stands for.

"You Can Always Remember If You N.E.V.E.R. F.O.R.G.E.T." is the story of Opooit and Nyack as told in a memory class with participants who have various memory concerns. Using the strategies that are "spelled out" in the story, each one finds success both personally and professionally.

My hope is that others will see that by following the examples of Nyack, Opooit, and the delightful people in Memory 101, they, too, can feel better about their memories and help their students.

ACKNOWLEDGMENTS

Many thanks go to my friends and family who supported this endeavor and endured my absences as I completed this project.

I want to thank the researchers who are working diligently to find the cures and preventions for diseases that affect our precious memories.

A special thanks to my extraordinary editor, Faye Zucker, for seeing Opooit and Nyack as disseminators of valuable information, for steering me in the right direction, and for being my friend.

Corwin Press gratefully acknowledges the contributions of the following reviewers:

Carrie Jane Carpenter
2003 Oregon Teacher of the Year
Hugh Hartman Middle School
Redmond, OR

Marguerite Lawler-Rohner
2004 Maine Teacher of the Year
Westcott Junior High School
Westbrook, ME

Burt Saxon
2005 Connecticut Teacher of the Year
Hillhouse High School
New Haven, CT

Linda Winburn
2005 South Carolina Teacher of the Year
Summit Parkway Middle School
Columbia, SC

Steven Wyborney
2005 Oregon Teacher of the Year
Nyssa Elementary School
Nyssa, OR

ABOUT THE AUTHOR

 **Marilee Sprenger** is a professional development consultant who has taught at all levels, from prekindergarten to graduate school. She is an adjunct professor at Aurora University, where she teaches brain-compatible strategies and memory courses. For the past fifteen years, she has been engaged in raising student achievement using brain-based teaching strategies, differentiation, and memory research. Marilee is a member of the American Academy of Neurology, the Cognitive Neuroscience Society, and the Learning and Brain Society, as well as many education organizations such as ASCD and Phi Delta Kappa. She is the author of *Learning and Memory: The Brain in Action, Becoming a Wiz at Brain-Based Teaching, Differentiation Through Learning Styles and Memory,* and *How to Teach So Students Remember.* She has written numerous articles and provides staff development internationally. Her passion is combining educational neuroscience with scientifically based educational research to create learning environments that will improve memory and raise student achievement.

INTRODUCTION

It is the first night of class. I am looking over the list of participants. Seven teachers are in the "extra" class I agreed to teach this semester. The other class I am teaching is full, and I agreed to teach another session. My colleagues are warming up to the idea that perhaps some information on memory would be helpful both personally and professionally. I like having small classes so that the participants get to know each other better, and I can give them individual attention. I am always amazed at how many people are worried about their memories. But, of course, I realize that the only reason I am teaching this "Memory 101" class is because at one time I thought my memory was in trouble.

Years ago, as those ugly words *middle age* started approaching—at a mere forty-five years old—I found myself forgetful. All the appointments I used to keep in my head and had never forgotten, the phone numbers, and the birthdays—they weren't gone, but I found myself having to look some up. And when I missed a doctor's appointment, I thought it was all over!

So, the research began. I've always been a teacher. I started out in kindergarten but found my niche with older students as I moved up to middle and high school before I started teaching at a nearby university. I really enjoy doing research and have always been happy with the results of that research: knowledge, confidence, and an "edge" in my work and my personal life.

The memory research is compelling. As we age, there may be a little decline in some areas, but nothing major (Bloom, Beal, & Kupfer, 2003). I discovered that my outlook on life and my attitude toward my memory could play a role in how well my brain and my memory work. I applied the simple principles with my students and within my personal life. When the school district asked me to offer a memory class for the teachers, I jumped at the chance to design Memory 101. The title comes from a course of the same name offered at Beth Israel Deaconess Medical Center, a teaching hospital affiliated with Harvard Medical

School (Haddock, 2001). I thought it would be a catchy title, and it certainly gets straight to the point. As educators, we should understand memory, so it's time for some of this background knowledge to be shared.

THE PARTICIPANTS

As I look at the list, I like the diversity: a P.E. teacher, a music teacher, two primary school teachers, a middle school language arts teacher, a high school science teacher, and a librarian. Dealing with memory problems and memory fears affects everyone.

"Okay," I think to myself, "if I want to assure these people that good memories are within their grasps, I'd better make sure that I know these names." I intentionally ask for a picture to accompany the registration. As a classroom teacher, knowing my students' names on the first day of school made them feel good about themselves and increased their confidence in me. I always studied the school yearbook each summer to learn the names of students in my incoming classes.

Gail Kilpatrick, a thirty-seven-year-old with shoulder-length blonde hair and high cheekbones, teaches high school science. She's afraid the periodic table of the elements will fade from her mind like so many other things! She is also concerned about her students forgetting information from one day to the next.

Jack Burns, a forty-seven-year-old P.E. teacher, has long dark hair and amazing blue eyes. Jack just started having memory problems.

Grace Jorgenson, fourth-grade teacher, has brown curly hair and wears rimless glasses. She's fifty-three and has short-term memory concerns.

Alice Belts has been a stay-at-home mom for twenty years, and now she is working as a librarian again. Alice can't remember where she puts things, and she's amazed at what the students forget.

Dr. David Schwarts, the music teacher for the high school, looks very professional with his silver hair around the temples and his horn-rimmed glasses. He has a soothing smile. David's forgetting appointments with students.

John Otis, a fair-haired middle school language arts teacher with blue eyes and a wicked smile, is fifty-two years old. He's been worried about his own memory for two years. He forgets what he just said and has to backtrack when he is giving students instructions. He is also disappointed in the test results he is getting from his students.

Ava Brophy is a beautiful African American woman who has been teaching third grade for thirty years. Ava finds herself missing appointments and misplacing her keys. She wants to be sure that she does nothing to jeopardize her students.

"I think I've got it," I say to myself as I prepare a small table with participants' names and a symbol to act as a mnemonic aid. "Okay, I'm ready. Will you join us?"

Ava	Grace	Alice	David	Jack	John	Gail	You
3	4	📖	🎵	🏀	🖼️	🔬	

CHAPTER ONE

MEMORY 101

*You Can Always Remember
If You N.E.V.E.R. F.O.R.G.E.T.*

Ava	Grace	Alice	David	Jack	John	Gail	You
3	4	📖	♪	🏀		🔬	

"Welcome to Memory 101!" I just finish preparing for my new students as they begin to arrive at 7:00 p.m. As is my habit with all students, I greet each at the door by name.

"Hello, John, I'm Marilee Sprenger. It's so nice to meet you."

John is a bit taken aback, but politely responds with, "Thanks, Marilee. It's nice to meet you, too."

I continue my personal greetings. The last person to enter, however, doesn't match any of the pictures I received with their registration. This woman has very dark hair, and I can't place her.

"Welcome to the Memory 101 class," I say. "You don't look like any of the pictures that were sent to me." With only seven people in the class, I realize that this should be Mrs. Kilpatrick, but she certainly doesn't look like the picture I have.

"I'm Gail Kilpatrick. I sent you an old photo of myself. I've changed my hairstyle and the color. I'm sorry if I confused you."

I carefully look at the face, smile, and shake Gail's hand. "It's very nice to have you here," I say sincerely as I turn to the rest of the class, "You can write this down: Connect a face to a name with features that stay the same. Don't try to remember who people are just by their hair. It can change easily. Bank robbers change their appearance in this way and often get away with their crimes."

I write this on the board. I turn back to face the group and the questions begin. "I signed up for this class because I heard it was a good one. I'm feeling a little self-conscious because it's so small. Are there others who are concerned about their memories? Or are we the only ones?" asks Jack.

"Yes. I want to know the answer to that, too. Plus, no offense to anyone, but I think I'm the youngest person here. Do young people take this class? Am I the youngest?" Gail wants to know.

"I'm only forty-two," quips Alice.

David jumps in with, "I'm forty-five. I don't think I'm that much older than Gail."

"So, am *I* the oldest person here?" Grace asks.

"Hang on, everyone. *I'm* the oldest person here," I interject. "Let me tell you about the people who sign up for this class. My youngest participant was twenty-six and in medical school. The oldest was eighty-two. I have had all ages in between since I started this program. The school district asked me to offer this class here at the school because the feeling was that some of you had memory concerns for your students as well as yourselves. Some of you have specific memory problems, while others just feel like you're 'slipping' in general. This is a class for everyone because most individuals know very little about how their memories work. My hope is to give you confidence, give you strategies, and give you the power to take control of your own memory as well as help your students. I've had many parents try to sign up their children for this class, but I feel it's made for adults and I'm not comfortable mixing the age groups. I thought about creating a Memory 101 for students, but I think if I can share this with the teachers, they can fill the needs of the students."

"Are you saying that my memory may work differently than Grace's?" asks Alice.

"That is exactly what I'm saying. You each have unique memories and your own way of storing them," I reply.

"Or not storing them," adds David.

The entire group laughs, and the stress levels lower in the process.

"Why don't we start with some examples of the problems you are having? I know that when I first started being concerned about my memory, I missed a few appointments."

The entire group nods with understanding and sympathetic smiles. "But you don't do that anymore?" queries David.

"That's right," I respond.

"You write everything down," Grace adds in a knowing way.

"I do have all my appointments in my Palm Pilot, but I don't always have to look."

The group seems impressed, and I urge them to start sharing. Alice is the first to tell her story:

"Well, after being at home for many years, I feel like I've forgotten how to function in the real world. I was always reminding my own kids about appointments, lessons, homework, and chores. If I forgot something, so did they—or so it seemed.

"Now, as a librarian, I have to remember who's holding what for whom. I have to remember when shipments are expected. I have to remember which teachers are bringing their students in which period, and the students expect me to know all their names. When someone asks for a book, I walk around the desk to help them, and by then I've forgotten what they asked."

There are knowing nods and a few comments like, "Been there, done that."

"Thanks, Alice. We all appreciate your sharing. Who would like to go next?"

Jack volunteers. "Okay. Here goes. I get up for the early-bird P.E. class, and I have to leave the house by 6:00 a.m. I'm finding myself forgetting to set my alarm. I'm spending precious time hunting for my car keys or my grade book. I get to school, and I'll forget some kid's name. I see these kids every day. This is scary!

"I never used to have these problems. I remembered everything!"

Everyone nods except David. I look at his apprehension and ask him to go next. He does.

"Well, I know you all have your concerns. I'm sure some of your situations may be embarrassing, but I have trouble keeping my in-school appointments straight. I teach private piano lessons after school hours, and I've missed two of those lessons in the last few months.

"We are getting ready for the school musical, and the principal caught me in the hall and asked which pieces I had selected. I stood there like an idiot. Great way to instill confidence with your administrator, huh? I walked back into my office where I had orchestrated the entire performance and I suddenly remembered. I was so relieved. But I have to make sure I don't do that again. I was certain that something was wrong with me."

As David finishes, the others grow quiet. I say, "I know many of you think you have the beginning stages of Alzheimer's or dementia. Those would be distressing, and I am not a clinician qualified to rule out those possibilities. I can tell you from my years of sharing memory information with others that none of my participants, to my knowledge, ever had one of those problems. They were all very much like you, with very similar stories. They left this class knowing they had to put some effort into their memories, but they knew that their memories were normal. Who would like to go next?"

Grace sits up straight, clears her throat, and begins. "I guess my problems are more like Jack's. Beyond that, I'm very concerned about my students. They forget from one day to the next. I know that my students are very young, but I can see that 'aha' moment on their faces one day, and the next they don't have a clue what I'm talking about. Does anyone else see this in their classroom?" Everyone nods.

"I feel like I'm always repeating myself, and I probably am! Not because I don't remember saying things, but rather because my students just don't get it! And yes, I'm worried about my memory, too. My students have to think that nothing gets by me. And lately, things *are* getting by me. I forgot my sister's birthday last week," Grace adds with a sigh.

"Oh, yeah, I've done that, too," quips Jack. "My whole family is probably mad at me for the important dates I forget!"

Ava is next. "I've been teaching for thirty years. At the same school. In the same grade. Is it any wonder I feel as if I'm repeating myself?" Everyone laughs.

She continues. "I have to admit, Marilee, that I wasn't completely honest on your questionnaire. Oh, I have short-term memory problems. But there's more. I've had to adapt to goals, standards, behavioral objectives, and benchmarks. I can do that. I've seen the pendulum swing from gifted to inclusion and now to No Child Left Behind. But what about me? I think I'm being left behind! I can't keep up with the technology. The electronic grade book, the Internet, e-mail, and instant messaging. My head just spins. I want to do a good job. I want to offer my students everything. But it just isn't fun anymore. I don't know how to remember all this new stuff!"

There are many nods of understanding. Before I can thank Ava, John breaks in. "I think my problem is completely different than anyone else's. My grade and content area is part of the testing program. My students get state tested, nationally tested, district tested, and any other testing that can be done. I'm getting pretty testy about the whole thing! I'm accountable for how my students do. I don't know how to teach anymore so that the students will remember what they need for the test. I have practically dropped my whole curriculum and now exclusively teach to one test or another. Can you help me?" John pleads.

I nod, "I know that each of you is struggling with your own mind. And I believe there are many things you can learn from this class that will make your memories better and help your students as well. Let's hear from Gail."

Gail squirms in her chair. "Well," she begins, "I feel as a teacher that I should really understand memory. Isn't that what I'm about—helping kids learn and remember? But the way things have been lately, I'm thinking of asking *them* for help!"

She pauses, and I encourage her to continue. "What are you noticing?"

"It all started when some former students stopped by at the beginning of the school year. I've always had great rapport with kids. I try to have a student-friendly classroom and lab. So, the students sometimes do come back to visit. Like I said earlier, I'm thirty-seven. I shouldn't be having memory problems yet!

"Anyway, these students show up at my door. I look up and smile. I am happy to see them . . . only I don't know whom I'm happy to see! I recognize that I had them, but I don't remember their names. I try to cover it up. I say, 'Hey, how are you? What are you two up to now?' They proceed to tell me which colleges they are attending, and I am racking my brain trying to think of names. It's not working, so I come up with a crazy idea. 'Say, why don't you two write a nice note on the board about this class—like how much you learned—and sign your names with the year you were here.' Thank heavens, they thought it was a great idea. They wrote the note, and the minute I saw their signatures, I felt like a dope. I knew exactly who they were, what period I had them, and where they sat.

"I was so relieved. But when they left, I was scared. What is wrong with my brain? Why can't I remember someone I saw every day for a whole semester or a whole year?"

The group becomes quiet as they look to me for answers.

"Your stories are unique to you. That's because each of us has a unique life and a unique brain. There are several lessons we can learn about memory. Once you understand them, I believe you will have power over your memory and have strategies to help your students with theirs. That may sound cliché, but it is true. In order to let you see how effort enhances our chances of remembering, we are going to study the wisest of animals."

"The owl?" Jack guesses. I shake my head.

"It must be the elephant. Elephants never forget, right?" asks Grace.

"My luck, if I were an elephant, I'd be Dumbo!" Jack quips.

"Grace is correct. I think I learned a lot about myself when I first heard this story. Listen and see what you think," I begin.

YOU CAN ALWAYS REMEMBER
IF YOU N.E.V.E.R. F.O.R.G.E.T.

Once upon a time, many, many years ago, in the jungle of Africa there lived the lion king, Nyack. Nyack was a very stately lion. He was eleven feet long from his nose to the tip of his tail. His beautiful mane was thick and luxurious. When Nyack walked through the jungle, he looked majestic, and many of the animals feared him.

One day, Nyack was strolling through the grasslands, as was his habit. He felt his job as king was a responsible position and that he must keep an eye on his land and its inhabitants. Besides, he was rather hungry and he thought perhaps he would spy a warthog for a midmorning snack.

In the distance, Nyack saw two zebras scurrying through the bush. He thought perhaps hunters were stalking them, but as he perused the area, he could see no danger. He continued his walk and almost stepped on some chimps that were scampering by. Nyack considered their flavor and decided not to pursue them.

As soon as the chimps disappeared, two mature giraffes came galloping by. Nyack's first thought was again of his hunger pangs. When he decided it was too nice a day to pursue an animal as large as a giraffe, he realized that all the animals he had passed—or who had passed him—were heading in the same direction. He wondered where they were going. The area they were heading toward was sometimes inhabited by a herd of elephants.

"Hmmm," he thought to himself, "a baby elephant might be a delightful morning treat!" So, he headed in that direction.

When Nyack came up to the clearing, he saw a curious sight. The animals that had passed him were standing and waiting in line to talk to an elephant! Nyack did not understand why they would do such a thing. He stood back and listened to the conversations.

"What do you want to know about?" one of the giraffes asked a chimp.

"I want to know what day the hunters are coming," answered one of the zebras.

"We are interested in knowing on what day the bananas will ripen," responded a chimp. "Why are you giraffes here? What do you want to know?"

"We're here to see if Opooit the elephant remembers where the tallest trees are with the sweetest leaves. We are very hungry today."

The chimps chuckled. "Of course Opooit remembers—elephants never forget!"

They were all nodding and laughing at the thought of Opooit forgetting anything. Nyack was not happy with these goings-on.

Suddenly Nyack roared. His roar can be heard for five miles, so you can imagine how loud and scary it sounded to the animals only a few feet away from him. They began to tremble.

"Why do you go to an elephant with such questions?" he continued to roar. "I am your king. You should come to me. I have all the answers."

The animals were ready to scramble away, but before they did, Morubisi, the wise old owl above them in a tree, began to speak.

"Whooo do you think you're kidding?" Morubisi asked of the lion. "You are only king because you are large and vicious. Animals are afraid of you. Would you answer these questions that the inhabitants of your kingdom ask? Are you capable of answering these questions? The squirrels are in line here. They have forgotten where they buried their nuts. Can you tell them?"

The trembling animals hesitated before running off. They wanted to hear the answers to Morubisi's questions.

Nyack coughed, as lions sometimes do when they have to think. The lion cough sounds like a low roar, and the sound keeps animals frozen in their tracks. Finally, Nyack spoke.

"I do not know where the squirrels hid their nuts. I am a busy king. I have many things to attend to." With that, Nyack walked away. For the first time, the animals saw him with his head bowed.

The animals relaxed and stayed in line waiting for Opooit to give them their much-needed information.

When the last of the creatures received their answers, Opooit thought it would be a good time for a nap. Just as he was preparing his bed, he heard some footsteps. He was surprised to see that Nyack was back. Opooit didn't know if he should greet him or run to protect his children. He chose to give Nyack the benefit of the doubt and waited for him to approach.

As Nyack got closer, even with poor elephant vision, Opooit could see that Nyack's head was down and he looked sad.

"What can I do for you, sire?" asked a respectful Opooit.

He watched as Nyack took off his crown and placed it on Opooit's table. "I am here to turn my kingdom over to you."

Shocked, Opooit raised his trunk and trumpeted. "I am not meant to be king of the jungle. That is your job."

"No," Nyack replied, "you are wrong. I cannot help my subjects as you can. You remember where they store their food. Without that information, they will not survive. You know when the hunters come. With that information, my subjects know when to hide and save their lives. You help them much more than I do. I do not deserve to be their king."

"But, Nyack," Opooit said, "you are the king. You protect your kingdom."

"I wouldn't have a kingdom to protect without you. You are more worthy than I. The kingdom is yours." With that, Nyack turned to leave.

Opooit began to think of all of the things he needed to do. He did not want this added responsibility. Opooit had a family to take care of. In times of need, Opooit had to travel far to see members of his kin.

Taking in a deep breath, Opooit announced, "I can help you remember all of this for your subjects."

Nyack turned and looked Opooit in the eye. "I am not a young lion, Opooit. My memory is not very good. Plus, I spend a great deal of time resting. I do not think you can help me."

"Oh yes, I can!" declared Opooit. "I can help you never forget!"

Nyack looked carefully at Opooit's home. On one of the trees was a sign that read N.E.V.E.R. F.O.R.G.E.T. He looked at the sign and back at Opooit. "Do you really believe you can teach this old lion how to remember so I can help my subjects?"

"I will teach you to N.E.V.E.R. F.O.R.G.E.T.," Opooit stated positively. "Come back tomorrow and we'll begin."

Nyack lifted his head up and walked back to his den.

"I think we've just about run out of time," I declare as I end the story.

"You mean you're going to leave us hanging here?" Ava asks disappointedly.

"I have a questionnaire I would like you to fill out. It will only take a few minutes. I would like you to keep it in your class notebook. By the end of this course, you will be able to determine why you answered yes to any of the questions and what you can do to help yourself. I also have a questionnaire that you can give your students.

"Taking control of your memory is a process. We'll learn the information and practice it over the entire course. I hope you'll take the opportunity to apply many of the concepts. For tonight, I would like you to reflect on the questions under 'Maintain Your Brain.' Next week we will begin to identify the first letter in N.E.V.E.R. F.O.R.G.E.T. Have a great week!"

MAINTAIN YOUR BRAIN

- Think about memory problems you may be experiencing. Which character's issues resemble yours? Why?
- Look over your class roster(s). List the memory difficulties you see in your students. Are they similar to yours? Do most of the students have the same memory problems?

(Text continues on page 15)

Figure 1.1   Memory Questionnaire for Adults

Circle the word that best describes each statement.

1. I forget names of people right after I am introduced to them.

   Always   Sometimes   Never

2. I miss appointments.

   Always   Sometimes   Never

3. I forget where I put my keys.

   Always   Sometimes   Never

4. I forget where I park my car in a large parking lot.

   Always   Sometimes   Never

5. I have trouble finding words when I speak.

   Always   Sometimes   Never

6. I forget important dates like birthdays.

   Always   Sometimes   Never

7. I forget what someone just told me.

   Always   Sometimes   Never

8. I forget directions.

   Always   Sometimes   Never

9. I forget what I just read.

   Always   Sometimes   Never

10. I forget what I was saying.

   Always   Sometimes   Never

Figure 1.2   Memory Questionnaire for Students

Circle the word that best describes each statement.

1. I forget to take my books and assignments home with me.

    Always   Sometimes   Never

2. I forget to do my homework.

    Always   Sometimes   Never

3. I forget information the teacher told me the day before.

    Always   Sometimes   Never

4. I forget my multiplication tables.

    Always   Sometimes   Never

5. I think I know some dance steps, but when I try to dance I don't remember them.

    Always   Sometimes   Never

6. I forget my friends' phone numbers.

    Always   Sometimes   Never

7. I forget to bring paper or pencils when I run out at school.

    Always   Sometimes   Never

8. I have to borrow items from others when I should have them with me.

    Always   Sometimes   Never

9. I go to movies and forget what I saw a few days later.

    Always   Sometimes   Never

10. I rarely remember what I read in a textbook.

    Always   Sometimes   Never

TRAIN THE STUDENT BRAIN

- Begin a conversation with your students about memory. Make a list of the types of strategies they know and use.
- Use the questionnaire with your class as a basis for discussion or journaling.

CHAPTER TWO

N = NOTICE

Intention Increases Retention

Ava	Grace	Alice	David	Jack	John	Gail	You
3	4	📖	♫	🏀	(portrait)	🔬	

At the second session, I see the seven participants resume their seats around the conference table. Pens in hand, they await a magic bullet just like the participants of every memory class I've taught. They are somewhat disappointed as I begin, "Now, be aware that there is no magic bullet. At least, not one that I can offer you. Science is working on brain pills, and I believe if you search you can find one to try. Short of that, I can offer you my suggestions based on recent memory research.

"It has been determined that we are bombarded with sensory stimuli constantly. Thousands of sights, sounds, and other messages that cannot possibly be stored are coming at us. Of those messages, neuroscientist Dr. Michael Gazzaniga believes we drop about 99 percent [1998]. Isn't that amazing?

"The reason is clear. Our brains are designed for survival. Therefore, they pay attention first to information that pertains to our ability to thrive. We get a message that we are hungry. It's hard to avoid that message, isn't it? A loud noise gets our attention quickly as it might be a threat.

"So, we must remember that 1 percent of our daily messages in the form of information, sights, sounds, and feelings are going to have our awareness. The rest will disappear. It's really a matter of what we deem important for our personal survival.

"Your brain is designed to forget. If we want to remember something we must make an effort. That is why you are here. You want to make an effort." I walk to the board and write

"Let's see what we can learn from our story, 'You Can Always Remember If You N.E.V.E.R. F.O.R.G.E.T.'"

A DAY TO REMEMBER

Nyack could hardly sleep as he looked forward to his meeting with Opooit. He was hoping he would be able to learn to remember all the vital information that the animals in his kingdom required. He was hoping he could remain king and feel successful.

When he arrived at Opooit's, he was anxious to start. "Okay, Opooit," he said, "How do I remember?"

"This is a process," Opooit replied. "We have to start at the beginning in order to NEVER FORGET. Take a close look at my sign. What do you notice?"

Nyack walked over to the NEVER FORGET sign. "I see that it says 'NEVER FORGET.' That's all."

"Notice more," commanded Opooit.

Nyack looked more closely at the sign. "Well, it looks like there is a period after each letter. It says N.E.V.E.R. F.O.R.G.E.T."

"That's exactly right. Those words are an acronym. That means that each letter stands for something else," stated Opooit.

"You mean like those people who show up with AWF on their trucks? The African Wildlife Foundation?" Nyack questioned.

"Yes. You've got it. Each of the letters in NEVER FORGET stands for a word or phrase. Elephants never forget because we are taught to N.E.V.E.R. F.O.R.G.E.T."

"So, once I know what they mean, I will never forget?" Nyack proposed.

"Not so fast, Nyack. I didn't learn to N.E.V.E.R. F.O.R.G.E.T. overnight. I had to understand and use each concept until it became natural for me."

Notice

"You mean like a habit?" asked Nyack.

Opooit raised his trunk and proclaimed, "That's just what I mean. Let's start with the N in N.E.V.E.R. F.O.R.G.E.T. The N stands for notice. Your first step is to start noticing things. I know where the squirrels hide their nuts because I notice them doing it. I notice when the hunters come and when the bananas ripen. I was taught from a very young age to notice things."

"Are you telling me to pay attention?" wondered Nyack.

"Yes. Keep your eyes and ears open. Observe things. Don't let the world pass you by. You will remember much more if you pay attention. As the humans say, 'Stop and smell the roses.' But more than that, notice where they are, how they grow, what they look like, and when they blossom."

"Okay," Nyack uttered, "N is for notice. What's next?"

"This is the end of the lesson for today. You have to go out and start to notice. At first, you will notice when you are noticing, but eventually you will automatically notice things."

Nyack was not happy that he had an assignment, but he really wanted to be the kind of king his subjects would respect and come to. He walked off slowly, turning his head to notice what he passed by.

"Just as Opooit stopped at this point with Nyack, I am going to stop here and send you off with an assignment," I announce.

"To stop and smell the roses?" Gail asks.

"More than that. You must intend to remember things. Notice with intent. Your brain will always attend to what is important. Determine what is important. Try remembering this:

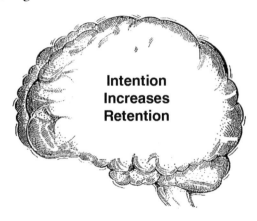

Intention Increases Retention

"There are times in our experiences when the only way we will remember is to be determined to do so. If you filled out your questionnaire from last week, take a look at it and determine if any of your problems are a result of not intending to remember. Most of what you are forgetting requires attention. If we intend to pay attention to where we put our keys, we will remember where they are.

"As a young teacher, I would be bitter about the mandatory staff development workshops I was forced to attend. I would bring other things to do and assume that the presenters were wasting my time. Then I became friends with a teacher who was appalled at my behavior at a workshop. She said to me, 'If you believe that your time is so valuable, you should be looking for information to take with you from this presentation. Don't waste your time. I always look for something helpful—and I've rarely been disappointed.' That really woke me up. From that time on, I paid more attention and intended to get something of value from every workshop. So intention can make a huge difference. Use the Eye Spy table [Figure 2.1] with your students, and use it yourself! Notice what's going on . . . you may be missing something memorable! Any questions? See you next time."

MAINTAIN YOUR BRAIN

- Are there times when you wish you had paid more attention to something? (The color of your friend's blouse, whether your mother's coat needed to be replaced, or the type of candy your boss eats?)
- Quiz yourself after you have been somewhere, like a restaurant. What kinds of people were there? What was your server's name? What was the conversation about?

TRAIN THE STUDENT BRAIN

- Quiz your students in the same way. Ask them to describe the lunchroom or what happened on the bus. Then ask them to tell you what they learned in geography last week. Why is there a difference? Talk to them about attention.
- Play Attention Bingo (see Figure 2.2) with your students. It will help with prediction, attention, listening, and memory.

(Text continues on page 23)

Figure 2.1   What Did You Notice Today?

Name: _____   Date: _____

Eye Spy
Today I Noticed . . .

What?	Where?	When?

Figure 2.2   Attention Bingo

Suggest the topic you are about to cover. After a brief discussion, have students fill in bingo spaces with possible ideas, concepts, and words that may be covered. Then read, lecture, show a video, and so on, and ask students to circle the words they wrote that are mentioned. Have small prizes like bookmarks, library passes, or pencils for those who get bingo. If no one "bingos," check to see who has the most circled and offer a prize.

		Attention Bingo Free space		

- Bring in some rocks or other small items that are associated with a topic you will study. Have students pick a rock and look at it for a minute. Then ask them to cover it and describe it to their neighbor. Have the students write down as many words as they know associated with rocks (i.e., Hard Rock Cafe, throw, etc.). Compare and read lists with other students. Then ask students to categorize their lists (possible rock categories might be types, sizes, colors, locations, etc.). Read some of your text or another book about the topic. Have students listen for their words and circle them as they are read. This activity encourages attention, helps with classification, and accesses prior knowledge.

CHAPTER THREE

E = EMOTE

Emotion Is the Potion

Ava	Grace	Alice	David	Jack	John	Gail	You
3	4	[book]	[music note]	[basketball]	[Shakespeare]	[microscope]	

I enter the classroom fifteen minutes early and am surprised to see John and Grace in their seats. They are chatting about something that looks humorous. As I greet them, they both look up with wide grins.

"Well, it looks like you two had a good week," I begin.

Moments later, Ava, Gail, David, and Alice arrive. Jack walks in a little after the starting time.

"I'm sorry. I noticed I was going to be late. But I also noticed that my wife thought I should attend to the kids and drop them off at their karate lessons."

Everyone laughs.

I begin with, "Last week we learned that the first letter of N.E.V.E.R. F.O.R.G.E.T. stands for Notice and that Intention Increases Retention. Your assignment was to make an effort to notice. How did it work out?"

John immediately starts, "I had an unusual encounter this week with the father of one of my students. As we were talking on the phone about some possible strategies, I repeated a few things back to him to be sure I had it right. He stopped for a second and said, 'Do you have CRS, too?' Now, I had no clue what he was talking about. I thought maybe CRS was a strategy I hadn't heard of. Boy, was I surprised when he told me. He said, 'CRS stands for Can't Remember Stuff. I've got it bad.' I was just so stunned, and by the way, very relieved, when he said he had it, too. This father is barely thirty years old! After that, my confidence grew. I remembered everything we talked about. I later got out my laptop and entered my notes from memory!"

The group applauds. I hear comments like, "Only thirty years old; I'm doing great compared to him," and "CRS—I'll have to tell my husband that's what I have!"

"That's a great story. Did anyone else find that intention leads to retention?"

Grace begins, "I found myself paying closer attention to my students when they asked and answered questions. I also kept a pad of paper handy so I could write things down. Just an anecdotal record of sorts. I'm beginning to realize that I sometimes don't pay attention when I need to. I want to know what is going on in each conversation in my room. What do they call that, divided attention?"

I respond, "Yes, when we divide our attention, we lose a lot of information. This is called the *cocktail party effect*. In a room full of people in conversation, like a cocktail party, we are able to select what we pay attention to. Our brain allows us to filter out the other conversations [Ngo & Bhadkamkar, 1998]. Remember that 99 percent of incoming stimuli will be dropped. So, divided attention is one of memory's worst enemies."

Grace continues, "I have to admit, when things became hectic, I had a terrible time trying to remember everything."

"I went to back-to-school night," Gail offers. "I must have met dozens of parents. But I remembered to attend to each one in order to remember. I shook their hands to slow things down. I repeated their names. I even noticed a few funny things about them. But I won't know until conferences or the chili supper if I succeeded in remembering. Any suggestions?"

"To tell the truth," I chuckle, "I do. Talk to the kids of the parents you met. Try to make a connection between the student and the parent. If you remember anything unusual or important from your conversation with the parents, repeat it to the student. The repetition may help you recognize them and recall their names next time."

Gail writes down the suggestion.

At this point, Jack speaks. "My intentions were good, but my methods were poor. On Friday we started a new game called volleytennis. It got to be a real mess. Kids thought they could spike at any time, which is against the rules. Since the net is low, I think some of the short kids felt like they finally had a chance to get back at the taller ones who have been spiking balls in their faces for years. My brain just couldn't keep up with the continuous need for direction and the constant need for discipline. I felt like a failure!"

"Give yourself a break here. Anytime we start something new, it takes a lot of our working memory to handle it. It's not in long-term memory yet. Once you know the game better and the kids have played it a few times, it will get much easier. The important point here, Jack, and all of you, is that you are aware that you need to make some effort. This is an important first step. How'd you do, Ava?"

"I haven't electrocuted myself, so I guess that's something. I'm making lists and I'm checking them twice. I'm paying special attention in order to remember by noticing and practicing. I'm checking off the steps I need for each software program. I think it's helping, but it's slowing me down."

David shifts in his seat uncomfortably. "I'm trying to give myself a break. You know, forgetting is easier than remembering, but I feel like people have higher expectations of me because I've got my doctorate. I'm supposed to remember everything."

"Whoa, there, fella," Gail retorts. "You get to collaborate with your colleagues. You can say to your students, or their parents, that you will get back to them. You have time to research. It's time people realized that teachers do not have to know everything on the spot."

"I guess you're right, Gail. I just feel like all my colleagues, the students, and especially the parents expect more than I am giving. Like I should have all the information at my fingertips, but I'm not able to do that. I must admit that I am noticing more. When people talk to me, I am doing better at giving them my full attention."

"That's great, David. Let's hear from Alice," I suggest.

"Well, I'm not a complete failure," Alice begins. "I started attending and focusing in order to remember. It worked from the back of the desk to the front of the desk. That is, when a student asked for a book or an author, I could remember twenty seconds later what they asked. I just had to repeat it over and over again. I was successful until someone interrupted me. Then I was in trouble."

I stand up and say, "Please remember this number: 458–6329." I then walk out the door. In twenty seconds I return. I ask them to repeat the number back to me in unison. They all do.

"How did each of you remember the number?"

John: "I wrote it down."

David: "I repeated it repeatedly!"

Jack: " I remembered it as four hundred fifty-eight and sixty-three hundred twenty nine."

Grace: "I pictured the keypad on the computer and remembered it with my fingers."

Gail: "This sounds silly, but I sang it to myself."

Alice: "I started thinking about my sister's phone number and I got confused."

I begin explaining to the group about how immediate memory works. "This is the process that is used to temporarily store information for about twenty seconds. If you don't do something to help yourself hold onto the information, it will be quickly forgotten. Researcher George Miller came up with the theory that we can remember up to seven items for this short period of time [Baddeley, 1999].

"That's why I gave you a phone number. Seven digits. Perhaps that is why so many things come in sevens. The seven deadly sins, *The 7 Habits of Highly Effective People*, the seven wonders of the world . . ."

"What about the Ten Commandments?" Jack asks slyly. "Do you suppose there's so much trouble in the world because we can only remember seven of them?"

After the laughter subsides, I continue. "You each used a different method of remembering that number. That's because sometime in our lives we were taught some memory strategies, and we still use the ones that were successful. We rely on them.

"Now that we know a bit more about memory, let's go back to Nyack and Opooit. Once we start noticing things, we are on our way to N.E.V.E.R. F.O.R.G.E.T."

CAN A LION SHOW HIS FEELINGS?

A few days later, Nyack went to see Opooit, who was cooling himself off by flapping his big elephant ears.

"I noticed that it is a very warm day," declared Nyack. "I also have noticed that the birds are singing. Not only that, but also I noticed that the zebras and the gazelles are staying close to the water. The snakes are not around, as I noticed that they are trying to stay cool in the water and underground." Nyack smiled.

Opooit stopped flapping his ears and trumpeted. "I think you've got it! You have been paying attention. How does all this make you feel?"

"I feel good about this. Noticing is something I can do. It is easy to get wrapped up in my own thoughts and needs, but I am now able to direct myself to other things going on in the world. I like noticing!"

"Then I guess it is time to continue with our N.E.V.E.R. F.O.R.G.E.T. lesson. We must look at the next letter: E. This E is for Emote. If you want to remember something, try to get a feel for it. Feelings attached to information and experiences make them easier to remember," Opooit proclaimed.

"I'm not sure what you mean, Opooit. Can you give me an example?" asked Nyack.

"Well, how did you feel about the birds singing? Did you listen to their song? Do you like the birds?"

Nyack didn't hesitate for a moment, "Now that I notice the birds singing, I love their music. It's fun to listen to them sing and talk back and forth. I find it amusing as well as peaceful."

"That's it!" shouted Opooit. "You notice something and then you notice how you feel about it. That's what the E for Emote is all about. We are always feeling something. Take the opportunity to notice and name your feelings about what you experience."

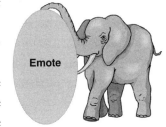

"This may be difficult, Opooit. I'm the king. I'm not supposed to show my feelings."

"You don't have to show them, although that would be nice. Just feel them. Notice what you notice and then notice how you feel. I will give you more information after you have mastered your emotions."

Nyack nodded and thanked Opooit. He walked away trying to take in his world and his feelings about it.

I stop my storytelling. "I'd like each of you to close your eyes. I want you to think back to your earliest memory. I mean really back as far as you can. Before you started kindergarten."

"I can't go back that far," says John. "How about first grade?"

"That will work," I reply. "Do you all have a memory in mind?" Everyone nods. "Would anyone like to share?"

"I will. Mine is horrible. I was little. Maybe five or six or seven. I wanted a kitten. I was pretty spoiled, so my folks got me one. I loved playing with him. His name was Troubles. I would run around the house and the kitten would chase me. One day I ran into the family room and jumped on a chair. The chair tipped back and fell . . . on Troubles. He didn't die right away, but he did die. It was awful. My sisters wouldn't let me think for an instant that I had caused it. But I did. I'll never forget it." Jack finishes his story with tears in his eyes. Several of the others are also in tears.

I leave the group in silence for a few moments. Then I ask for another volunteer. Perhaps someone with a happier memory.

"Okay. Mine is lighter. I remember losing my mom's ring in the backyard. She had taken off her wedding band while doing dishes and left it by the sink. I went into the kitchen, picked it up, and tried it on. Of course, it was way too big. Just as I was doing this, my sister came by and 'tagged' me and said, 'You're it!' With that, she ran outside and I ran after her. In all the chasing and tagging,

I must have dropped the ring. When the game was over, I remembered that I had had it on, but it was gone. I was crazed. I must have been seven or eight. My heart is racing just talking about it. It took about an hour, but we finally found it. My mom never knew!" Grace announces.

"I remember learning to ride a two-wheeler. It was awful. My dad was holding on . . . and then he wasn't. I crashed into the back of our car. I cut my lip so badly that I had to have stitches," David declares.

"I remember how excited I was for my first day at school. Then my mother left. I screamed for hours. I hated school for a while, but then I got over it." This was Gail's story.

Ava jumps in with, "The first day of first grade, my neighbor was playing on the monkey bars and fell and broke his arm. The bone was sticking out . . . it was so disgusting!"

The others tell similar stories. Then I ask, "Okay, what is parallel about these stories?"

"Well, I think Opooit gave it away. They are all emotional," offers Alice.

"Exactly. Our earliest memories remain with us because they brought out strong emotions in us. So do you see why this *E* for Emote is important?"

"I get it, but there are lots of things that I notice that don't evoke strong emotions," says Ava.

"You're right. But if there is something important that we want to remember, we can add some emotion. We can associate it with a song, a person, or a place that has emotional ties for us. In the psychology class I taught last semester, I had a participant named John Maxwell. There were two other young men named John. But Maxwell is my cat's name. I made that emotional connection and although I mixed up the other two Johns, I always knew John Maxwell. Does that make sense?" I ask.

"Is our next assignment to go out and notice with feeling?" asks Jack.

"Yes. Remember: Intention Increases Retention, and

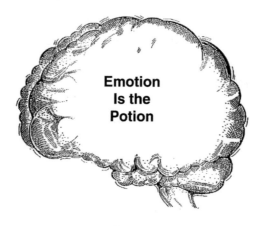

**Emotion
Is the
Potion**

"Dr. Dan Schacter, author of *The Seven Sins of Memory* [2002], states, 'Everyday experience and laboratory studies reveal that emotionally charged incidents are better remembered than nonemotional events.' Think about your students. Would adding emotion to your lessons increase their memories? Take a look at the Emotional Hooks chart. What do you already do that's emotional, and what could you do in addition? Look at your lessons for the next week. See if you can add some emotion and notice if there are any changes in your students."

"Have a great week!"

MAINTAIN YOUR BRAIN

- Are you doing better with noticing? What have you noticed that you usually don't?
- What mnemonic devices do you use to remember such things as phone numbers?

TRAIN THE STUDENT BRAIN

- Adolescents respond well to emotion because of the changes in their brains. This may be a good way to get their attention.
- Try the emotional hooks in Figure 3.1 with your students.

Figure 3.1   Emotional Hooks for the Classroom

Emotional Hooks

Strategy	Description	Example
Music	Find appropriate music to fit the theme or standard you are teaching.	World War II: "Yankee Doodle Dandy."
Personalization	Make content meaningful through prior experiences.	Weather: Share your experiences with inclement weather.
Storytelling	In any content area, some students may have no prior knowledge. Allowing those who have prior knowledge to share their experiences may provide the hook that students need to connect to new information.	Agriculture: In an urban area, many students may be unable to relate to this until they hear someone else's story.
Empathy	Specifically ask students to step into someone else's shoes.	Thomas Edison: How would you feel if your inventions didn't work?
Debate	Have students work in pairs to prepare their "side" of the situation.	Ethics: Is it okay for Jack to have stolen from the giant?
Role-play	Have students "pretend" they are in various situations related to content.	Students reenact the writing and signing of the Constitution.
Agree/Disagree Statements	Make a list of ten or more statements regarding your content that your students can choose to agree or disagree with. They will be emotionally involved when they give their opinions.	Biology: Male brains are larger than female brains.
Emotions Are Contagious	Act excited, upset, angry, and so on about the content you will cover.	Geometry: "I have been told that understanding angles is a waste of time. Do you believe that? I don't. Let's find out!"

CHAPTER FOUR

V = VISUALIZE

A Picture in Your Mind Creates
a Memory You Can Find

Ava	Grace	Alice	David	Jack	John	Gail	You
3	4	📖	🎵	🏀	🖼️	🔬	

It is the fourth night of class, and I wonder if my participants are getting the idea. So far, they've covered Notice and Emotion from N.E.V.E.R. F.O.R.G.E.T. It did seem that everyone worked on Notice, but I question how well they will do with the emotional part. It is by far the most powerful memory system to use, but it is not always easy to attach an emotion to an experience (Sprenger, 1999). My thoughts are interrupted when the entire class shows up at the same time.

"Looks like we all remembered to come!" laughs John.

"I have to share something," David insists. "When I left class last week saying 'emotion is the potion,' I felt pretty stupid. I even thought of dropping the class. But I turned on the radio; I had the 'oldies' station on. The song they were playing was 'In My Life' by the Beatles. That is one of my favorite songs, and I had the high school band learn it. I had a student the first year I taught it who was terminally ill. He was a teenager who loved the Beatles. Before he slipped into a coma, he asked for that song to be played continuously. His parents asked me to have the band play it at his funeral, which of course we did. I started crying when I heard the song on the radio. I started to change the station, and before I made contact with the dial, memories started flooding my brain. I remembered his name, the family members' names, his hospital room with the posters all over, his stereo, and one stuffed teddy bear that was on the windowsill. Then I remembered the last conversation I had with him, and that teddy bear sitting on his coffin."

Now several people are close to tears. David looks at them and apologizes. "I didn't mean to upset anyone. I want to share with you how powerful emotion is. That song is my memory connection to him. I am amazed at how many details I remember through that song and my sadness. So, I am absolutely sold on emotion as a potion . . . it's like a memory pill! Even though high school teachers are supposed to remain somewhat aloof, I am going to try to make an emotional connection with each of my students. It will probably help all of our memories!"

Grace nods and speaks, "That's an incredible story, David. I made it my goal to create a personal connection with everyone I talked to. I realized that the conversations I remember best left me with a good or a bad feeling. I decided that I wanted to give my students and colleagues, as well as myself, something to remember. Whether I arranged to speak with someone or if it was by chance, I was sure to draw out some kind of emotion. I had to slow down to do this. I mean, I usually get straight to the point with people. Give them the answers, offer directions or suggestions, and move on. But I took time to notice how they sounded and key in on the emotion they were expressing, and made sure to try to get them to feel happy or happier by the time we finished. It worked great, and the best part was that I remember every conversation!"

I cannot hide my satisfaction. "I'd like you to think about our previous classes. Can you summarize in your head what we did? Are there details you remember? Do you know how you felt each session?

"From your nods and smiles, I am going to assume that you all have pretty strong memories of our work together so far. Can anyone tell me why?"

"That's easy," says Jack. "It is all emotional. I mean, this whole situation is emotional to us. It means a lot to each of us to figure out how our memories work, right? So we are approaching this class on an emotional level."

"Exactly," I affirm. "Just like the memories you shared today. We hold on to our emotional memories very well. I try to keep my classes committed on an emotional level because I know this class wouldn't be very popular if you didn't remember much of what we did!"

Gail interrupts the laughter. "I have to tell you what I did. I wanted to see if I could make the school day more memorable for my students and me. We are studying the central nervous system, and I wanted to make a big impact on the class. I got a realistic-looking mouse and put it in my desk before the students arrived. As I was beginning to talk about the nervous system, I opened my drawer as though I were getting a marker. I grabbed the mouse and tossed him out of the desk and screamed as though it were a total surprise. All the students gasped or screamed, because they thought it was real. I picked it up to show them my trick. Some were angry, but most were just relieved. I had them check their heart rates and we talked about our system's fight or flight response. It was a great opening to the topic. I know they'll remember the experience."

"It sounds like the emotion potion is working. Anyone else want to share?" I ask.

"I tried something at the library," Alice begins. "When students ask about an author or a book, I ask them why they are interested. I get some personal information that connects me to the topic, and I have no trouble remembering what I'm looking for!"

Ava jumps in, "That's kind of what I did. I've begun to personalize my interactions with students, family, and friends. For instance, a student was having some problems with a math assignment. I asked her how she felt about the topic and what memories it helped her access. Once she started talking about her prior experiences, the whole assignment made more sense to her."

"Well, I tried to add emotion in P.E. class without all the overcompetitiveness," begins Jack. "It's not easy. I can get kids to perform because they want to beat someone or prove something. That's emotional and I guess it's memorable, but it's not always productive. Remember, in physical education class, it really is not who wins or loses, but how they learn to play the game! What I've started doing is videotaping some of the games we play. For instance, we are working on volleyball right now, so I'm taping the games one day, and we review them the next. I make it as nonthreatening as I can. I edit the tapes so we don't see awful bloopers, just some attempts that could use improvement. The students love it, and now they have the opportunity to talk about the sport. So, I've added Notice to what we're doing as well."

"I guess I'm last," begins John. "The day after class last week, we were having Writer's Workshop. I decided I needed to try this emotion suggestion. I got all the kids writing and then called each student to my desk for a writing conference. I started with emotional questions: 'How are you doing today?' 'Do you have a lot going on with your other classes?' 'How is the writing going?' 'Do you feel as though you have a handle on the topic?' I know it sounds like just a list of questions, but most students interacted and answered each one. Even if we didn't talk much about their writing, I felt as if I had made a connection with the students. And I think they liked the contact. What amazed me was that several days later I would see a student in the library or in the hall and I would remember what they were writing about!"

"There is research supporting teacher-student interaction as a way to boost student achievement [Glasgow & Hicks, 2003]," I offer. "You and Ava may be doing much more than increasing memories."

"The Emotion Potion appears to be helpful to everyone. That is not true of all memory strategies. We have to pick and choose what works best for each of our unique minds," I state.

"I do have a question," says Grace. "Are elephants really smart? I thought dolphins were the smartest creatures after humans."

"That's a great question. Actually, elephants are very smart. They are often compared to dolphins in their abilities. Perhaps their tricks aren't as cute and clever as dolphins, so they don't get the attention. Any other questions before I begin?"

The group is silent, so I launch into the story.

NYACK GETS THE PICTURE

Several days later, while Opooit was out checking on his herd, he heard some sobbing coming from the bushes. He cautiously approached, not wanting to intrude on anyone. Much to his surprise, he found King Nyack wiping his eyes with his tail.

"Are you all right, sire?" he asked.

Nyack looked up and said, "You know, Opooit, this is all your fault. I started letting myself feel, and here I am in tears. I noticed that one of the squirrels was hit by a rock and was having trouble getting up a tree. I thought about what you said about feeling things. I wondered how it would feel to help my subject. I had him crawl up my tail and onto my head. From there, he could get to a low branch. I started to walk away, and he called me back and said, 'Oh, King Nyack, that was the nicest thing anyone ever did for me. You are a great king.' I thanked him and walked away. I knew I was going to cry, and I didn't want anyone to see me. I'll never forget the experience."

Opooit smiled. "It looks like you are beginning to understand how noticing and emotion can help you."

"Yes," responded Nyack, "but I don't want to stop here. I want to learn the rest of N.E.V.E.R. F.O.R.G.E.T., so I can be the king that my kingdom needs."

"Then let's go on to the next letter: V. V stands for Visualize. This is another strategy that can be very potent. When you want to remember something, you get a picture of it in your mind. Sometimes this takes practice, but it can be great fun. What did you have for dinner last night?"

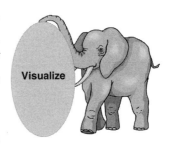

Visualize

Nyack cocks his head and says, "I had a warthog."

"What went on in your mind to help you come up with the answer? What did you first think of?" Opooit quizzed.

"I thought about where I was last night. I was in a clearing by the river and one of the lionesses killed the warthog and brought it there. It was very tasty, as I remember."

"You see, you visualized where you were. When you thought of the place, the details came back to you. That's the power of visualization," concluded Opooit.

"So I should try to remember what things look like?" Nyack asked.

"Yes. You helped a squirrel today. Can you picture him climbing up your tail? Can you see him in the tree?"

"I can," said Nyack. "Okay. You've been helpful so far. I'll see if I can get a picture of what happens so I can remember it."

And off he went.

I stop the story and say, "At our first session, David gave us an example of a memory problem that was connected to a place. Information that he knew easily slipped his mind . . . until he went into his office. You see, the memory was associated with a context or location: the office. This type of memory is called *episodic*. Episodic memories are associated with events and locations [Bourtchouladze, 2002]. David's memory was in that room. Just as dinner is associated with a place."

"Wow!" exclaimed David, "You're right! But I need those memories outside that room . . . so I should visualize the room to access those memories?"

"Visualization—creating a picture of what you want to remember—is one of the most compelling memory strategies [Sprenger, 2005]. Let me demonstrate. I want you all to make a list of words for me to remember. It can be a grocery list or contain any word you want. It is best if I know the definition of the word. David, you write the words on the flip chart as people offer them to you. They can give the words in any order; in other words, Grace may call out 'broccoli—number one.' I will turn my back so I cannot see the list. When you finish, I will give the words back to you in any order that you wish. We can make a ten- or twenty-word list, but looking at the clock, I think we should just do ten."

The group begins offering words for the list. In just a few minutes, there are ten items on the list.

1. ham

2. sushi

3. love

4. peanut butter

5. PowerPoint

6. lipstick

7. watermelon

8. napkin

9. briefcase

10. laryngitis

I ask the group how they would like the words repeated. They ask for the list backward. I am able to accurately associate each word with its proper number. They applaud.

"How did you do that?" they all ask.

"Not only am I going to share my secret, but also you are all going to be able to do this trick before you leave tonight. First of all, this is a visualization technique. The idea is to use as many senses as possible to get a 'big picture' of the item. But first you have to know the association technique. I used a rhyming peg system that goes like this:

One   = sun

Two   = shoe

Three = tree

Four = door

Five = hive

Six   = sticks

Seven = heaven

Eight = gate

Nine = line

Ten   = hen

"I associated each word in the list with its proper number. So, number one was ham. I pictured a ham with arms and legs putting on suntan oil as it sat in the sun! Two was sushi. I pictured sushi on my feet instead of shoes. Using more than just vision, I imagined how it would feel to have salmon and seaweed wrapped around my feet."

I share my other visualizations and then make a list for the group. They apply the peg system, and everyone remembers the entire list. "This is called a *mnemonic* device. Anything you use to help you remember is a mnemonic."

"Like the rhymes that you give us to go with each letter of N.E.V.E.R. F.O.R.G.E.T.," Alice adds.

"Exactly," I reply. "Any cue that assists you in never forgetting is a mnemonic. They're fun and easy."

"I can't wait to try this with my students," Gail says excitedly. "They're going to think I'm magic. Then I'll let them think they're magic by teaching them the trick. Are there others?"

"I think we have time for one more: the system of loci or location [Hagwood, 2006]. This has been around a very long time. Picture your bedroom as you look in the doorway. What is the first item to your left? Mine is a dresser that becomes number one. Next is a mirror; that's two. On the other side of the mirror is a closet door; it's three. Four is my desk. Five is a picture of my kids. Six is the window. Seven is the bed. Next is the bathroom; it's eight. Nine is a plant, and ten is a chair. If you have labeled ten things in your room with numbers, you have a peg system associated with a room you know well. You can remember items in order just as we did with the rhyming peg."

"Is visualization the way to remember people? Like what you learned the night of the first class?" Ava asks.

"Yes. Does anyone remember that rule?" I inquire.

"Connect a face to a name using features that stay the same!" squeals Gail. "I can't believe I remember it!"

"Good work, Gail, and the rhyme to help you remember to visualize is this:

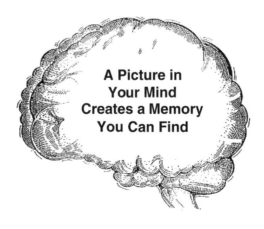

A Picture in
Your Mind
Creates a Memory
You Can Find

"Is there an easy way to do this with names?" Alice wants to know.

"There are books that have been published with name strategies [Hagwood, 2006]. The trick is to take someone's name and create a visual of it. The crazier it is, the better. Why don't you get in groups and try to create visuals for your names now?" I suggest.

The groups work for several minutes, and finally it's time to share.

Jack starts, "Alice and I worked together. To remember Alice Belts, I changed it to A List of Belts, so I can picture a piece of paper with dozens of belts on it. Does that work?"

"Remember, Jack, this is personal. If it works for you, it works," I propose.

Alice responds, "I think you're right. For Jack Burns, I thought of Jack as money. Then it was easy, I pictured those gorgeous bills burning. It's kind of sad."

"Again, the more bizarre it is, the more memorable it will be," I remind them.

Grace, David, and John worked together. David begins, "For Grace Jorgenson, John and I thought Greasy Jar Ginseng. So, the visual is a jar that is covered with grease and inside is ginseng tea."

Everyone nods at this and John steps up to the plate, "We changed David to Dave and then to dove. Schwarts was hard for us, so we just went to the ending. We have a dove with warts!"

At this everyone laughs, but then they agree that it is a good visual.

"Well, how'd you do with John?"

"John is easy," Grace begins. "We picture a toilet. For Otis, we thought of some pretty disgusting ideas, like odorous. But I don't think I want to visualize an odorous toilet. I suggested we stick with ode. From there we went to ode to toilet, and that took us to eau de toilette. John went from being a stinky toilet to perfume!"

"Even though you used several steps, the visuals can be reused. The name John may always bring to mind a toilet, and Jack may always be money," I suggest.

"Ava Brophy became a trophy. Oops, sorry about the rhyme! Ava sounds like 'I have a.' So, the visual is someone holding a trophy and saying, 'I have a trophy,'" Gail announces.

Then Ava adds, "From Gail Kilpatrick, we pictured a storm (gale) killing pets that do tricks. So, I see a dog being carried out to sea as he jumps to catch a Frisbee."

"I think you should all give yourselves a round of applause. This is a strategy that must be practiced. After an introduction, we can't stop and say, 'Excuse me, could I have ten minutes to try to remember your name? However, I have been known to go to the bar or sweets table at a party, look carefully across the room at someone I have met, and try to visualize their name . . . if I remember it! It is actually fun.

"Educational research is leaning toward teaching students more visualization skills. This falls into a category called nonlinguistic representations, that is, representing information without words. Many students do quite well with this [Marzano, Pickering, & Pollack, 2001].

"A rather exciting possibility is the use of *mind maps* [Buzan, 2003]. This is a concept developed in the 1970s in England by a man named Tony Buzan. It's a way to take notes or make lists. There has been some research showing how dyslexic students can benefit from using mind maps [Kenyon, 2002]. The strategy involves color and symbols. Words may be used if desired. I teach this strategy to my students. Let me write the simple steps."

1. In the center of a piece of paper, write your topic and put a circle or cloud around it.

2. Draw lines from the cloud on which to place a detail. You may write key words or just draw a symbol or picture.

3. Use different colors for each line.

4. Limit the number of lines or details that you include. (Remember the magic number seven?)

5. Be creative.

"I have begun a mind map about the concepts we have covered so far in N.E.V.E.R. F.O.R.G.E.T.

"As you can see, these can be used in many ways. I often make a mind map for my husband when I want him to go to the grocery store. I make each line an aisle. That way, he doesn't have to run back and forth getting items. I also use it for my presentations," I say.

"I use webs with my students. Is that the same thing?" asks Gail.

"Similar, but different. Any graphic organizer can help you form a visual of information. There are many kinds of organizers. You don't have to use someone else's ideas. Create your own. Mind maps become personalized [see Figure 4.1]. Any kind of picture or symbol that you will remember will work. Color may mean something to you as well. So, keep your visualizations colorful.

Figure 4.1   Beginning of a Mind Map

For instance, red is my favorite color. If something is important to me, I may visualize it in red to help me remember. Design your own system.

"I want to leave you with one more thought. Think of photos you have at home. I've heard them called visual mnemonics—a recapturing of memories through nonverbal means [Burmark, 2002]. Photos have stories behind them. The brain loves to think in stories [Damasio, 1999]. We remember stories better than simple facts or concepts. Go home and look at a few of those pictures and see how memories come flooding back. I hope your week is 'picture perfect'!"

MAINTAIN YOUR BRAIN

- Many adults think they are "giving in" by using graphic organizers, lists, or visuals to help them remember. Decide in what area your memory seems weak: appointments, grocery items, social events, names, and so forth. Think about what visuals might help you in any of these areas.
- Try a mind map for your next lesson plan. If it's new content to you, it will be a quick way to keep yourself on track without the students noticing that you are using notes.

TRAIN THE STUDENT BRAIN

- Many of your students are visual learners. It is important that we support the visual modality because the educational system and society are dependent on visuals. Use What's Your Visual Quotient? in Figure 4.2 to determine how well your students can visualize.
- If they have a low visual quotient, provide activities to help them become more visual. I suggest the Pictionary game, charades, and even twenty questions.

Figure 4.2   Increasing VQ

What's Your Visual Quotient?

For each question, circle the letter of every answer that applies to you.

1. After I see a movie, I remember
   a. the costumes that were worn and can describe them easily.
   b. the faces of the characters and can describe them easily.
   c. the scenes that were funny and can describe them easily.
   d. the action scenes and can describe them easily.

2. When I go to a friend's house, I notice
   a. the color of the carpet, wallpaper, and other decorations and can describe them easily.
   b. my friend's room—how it is arranged, the kind of equipment in the room—and what my friend was wearing, and can describe them easily.
   c. what the outside of the house looks like and can describe it easily.
   d. the route that I take to get there, including the landmarks, and can describe it easily.

3. When I want to recall information from a book, I picture
   a. the photos or illustrations on the page and can describe them easily.
   b. the pictures I created in my mind as I read.
   c. the characters in a story and can see them performing the actions and can describe them easily.
   d. where I was when I read the book, and then I can recall the information and can describe it easily.

4. When I am asked to draw, I approach the project by
   a. picturing what I want to draw in my mind.
   b. sketching out my ideas and then refining them as I see what they look like.
   c. creating new ideas that I imagine as I work.
   d. recreating the works of others as I remember them.

(Continued)

Figure 4.2 (Continued)

5. If I were a teacher, I would use the following types of visual information:
   a. video clips
   b. artists' renditions of the content
   c. charts and maps
   d. posters

Add up the number of circled items. This indicates how easy it is for you to visualize.

Scoring:

15 – 20   Your visualization skills are excellent and well practiced. Help others become as skillful as you!

10 – 15   You are a strong visual learner. Examine your areas of weakness and work on honing your skills.

5 – 10   You have many of the skills required to become a strong visual learner. Prioritize those areas of weakness and work on them.

1 – 5   You may have a strong preference for either auditory or kinesthetic learning. But this will not prevent you from increasing your visual skills.

Ideas for increasing your visual quotient:

1. Practice noticing and visualizing familiar places and things.

2. Try communicating with a friend through visual means.

3. Draw a diagram of your bedroom.

4. Look at pictures for a few minutes, put them away, and then try to picture them in your mind or recreate them on paper.

5. Draw definitions of vocabulary words.

6. Play Pictionary.

CHAPTER FIVE

E = EXERCISE AND EAT RIGHT

Body and Brain Are Yours to Train

Ava	Grace	Alice	David	Jack	John	Gail	You
3	4	📖	🎵	🏀	🖼️	🔬	

The seven memory seekers are eager to share at session five.

Jack begins, "I had some success with the location system. I used my office and went around the room designating areas. The desk is first, then a file cabinet, then a tall stool, and so on. I made sure I had that visual memorized. Then I waited to get busy. And of course, I had a note from the office asking for some paperwork by lunchtime. I looked at my desk, which was already covered with papers, and I imagined my lunch—sandwich, chips, and soda spilled all over the papers. Then Missy, one of my students, came in with a note from her mother: 'Could you please send home Missy's assignments for tomorrow as we must attend a funeral in Chicago?' I looked at the file cabinet. I pictured a hearse with schoolbooks pouring out the door. As I checked my lesson plan book, I realized that I had to collect the student emergency cards before the end of the day. I pictured the stool with an emergency technician performing CPR on a dummy. Well, it worked! Before I left for lunch, I pictured my desk and grabbed the paperwork I needed. After lunch, I wrote out Missy's assignments after I looked at the file cabinet. And I just pictured the stool and saw the 'emergency' and collected the cards. It was great!"

John was next to offer, "I tried mind mapping. I wanted to see if it was a good tool for my students. We are going over the elements of the short story, so I decided to mind map those. Now, most language arts teachers will tell you that students have a heck of a time remembering these elements, so I wasn't expecting miracles. As we mapped them together, I noticed that the students were laughing and talking about the symbols they chose, so I figured it was going to be helpful for their memories to have the emotional interaction. The next day, I asked them to recreate their mind map of the elements, and most of them could do so without asking or looking at the previous map! I think this is a strategy I will use often.

"I am trying to get my students to use visualization as well. When we read a story or a piece of nonfiction, I ask them what they 'see,' and I think it's beginning to take hold. Some of them are beginning their comments with, 'I see,' or "I imagine that . . .' It's pretty exciting!" John concludes.

"I also used mind maps . . . for my lesson plans," Gail begins. "I found that writing the words in colors allowed me to take a mental picture of the map, so I used very few symbols. It worked well. I created the map on Monday night. The lesson took three days. The only time I had to look at the map was to check to see if I was beginning in the right place before class. I had three different classes for this lesson, and I didn't end up in the same place each time. You know, different kids, different questions. I like the strategy, and because it helped me so much, I am going to teach it to my students as a note-taking strategy. I think it will really help them prepare for tests."

"The rhyming peg worked for me," Grace announces. "I tried it with teaching the names of the presidents just to see how my students would handle it. I taught them the rhyming peg on Tuesday. We reviewed it twice that day and twice the next. On Thursday, I began with the presidents and asked them to attach each one to the peg. They loved it! And they all did very well. For instance, for George Washington, the students came up with George cutting down the cherry tree with the sun beating down on him. We are making president picture books, so they are adding their peg picture of each president."

Ava speaks up. "I did it differently. I imagined myself going through the steps to boot up the computer, get Internet access, and do a search. I read the instructions that I had several times. Each time, I pictured myself doing it. Then, when I got to the computer lab, I walked over and began. It was amazing how well it worked. Is this an acceptable way to use this information?"

I respond, "If it works for you, it's more than okay. It's great. Research has shown [Gordon & Berger, 2003] that athletes imagine themselves performing and it actually improves their skills!"

"When someone asked for a book that I have read or know something about, I pictured a scene from the story," says Alice. "Then I carried the image wherever I had to go. It worked well until someone asked me for a book I hadn't heard of. I changed my tactic. The title was *Cunningham's Encyclopedia of Wicca in the Kitchen*. I know that has something to do with a type of faith related to witchcraft, but I don't know much about it. The funny thing is that when I was a kid, we had a dog named Wicka. I pictured Wicka, the dog, reading an encyclopedia in my kitchen. It was the strategy we used with our names last time. It worked great, except I think I was making too much noise in the library as I chuckled at the image in my head!"

"David, you've been quiet. Did you have any luck?" I ask.

"I'm sure it works well for some people, but I had better luck with the emotions and intention. I am trying to get my students to visualize themselves playing their instruments, and that appears to be working for some," he shares.

"Visualization can take time for some people, and there are those who don't enjoy it as much as others. If you are interested, you might try drawing a picture and seeing if you can remember it, but don't worry—there are plenty of other strategies for you. Let's continue the story and see what we can learn," I suggest.

THE LION'S SHARE

"How are you today, King?" asked Opooit as Nyack approached him.

"I am fine. Thank you, Opooit," replied Nyack, "I have had a wonderful visual experience. A lion's brain must have been made for images. I was walking along the riverbank three days ago. Two of my lion cubs were following me. They are both very young and cannot go far from the pride without an escort. I thought I would show them around the kingdom. I gave them quite a tour, or so I thought. When I returned to the rest of the family, the cubs were not behind me. I lost the kids! Their mothers were not very happy with me. I started to panic at the thought of them being eaten by a hippopotamus or rhinoceros, but then I reviewed my tour in my head. I pictured the riverbank, the babbling brook, and the grasslands. I could not see how I would have lost them in any of those places. Then I pictured the bush and the trees I had to worm my way through. I knew then that this was where the cubs would be. I ran to the spot, and there the two were, wrestling on the ground. They had been unable to keep up, and I hadn't been taking care of them. I learned two lessons. One: Keep noticing the kids. Two: Noticing and remembering a picture of where you are can be a lifesaver! Thank you, Opooit, for the visualization technique. Don't tell the giraffes, but I saw some very tall trees with fine leaves on them. I memorized the location with the hills and the stream beside them. If the giraffes need a good eating spot, I will be able to help them!"

Opooit was thrilled that N.E.V.E.R. F.O.R.G.E.T. was working so well for Nyack. He hoped he would be optimistic about the next letter.

"What's next, Opooit?" Nyack asked.

"E is the next letter. It stands for two important components of memory: Exercise and Eat Right," Opooit replied.

"Exercise! What does that have to do with never forgetting? I am a king. I don't exercise. Besides, I walk around noticing all the time. Isn't that enough exercise?" Nyack complained.

"Sire, you wanted me to teach you what works for never forgetting. This is part of it. It is very important to keep blood circulating throughout your body and your brain. Exercise is important to keep you healthy. Your ancestors are notorious for lying around almost twenty-one hours a day. That may be why you have memory problems. Now, I want you to start slowly. Instead of walking around just three hours a day, slowly add a half hour each day until you are up and moving more than you are down. When it is not too hot, do a little running. That will really help your mind and your heart."

"And, Eat Right? That seems a bit silly. The lionesses do the hunting, and I eat whatever they bring home. Shouldn't you be talking to them about this?"

"Well, sire, you choose what and how much you eat, don't you? You need to understand nutritional needs, so you can make good choices."

"I eat wildebeest, impala, zebra, giraffe, buffalo, and wild hogs when they are available. If not, I eat smaller animals like hares, birds, and reptiles. This is what my ancestors ate; therefore, this is what I eat."

"Believe me, sire, I eat hundreds of pounds of food each day. What we have discovered, though, is that we should eat no more than is necessary. Animals that eat fewer calories live longer than animals who consume too much."

"I should walk around hungry? How will I be able to notice and remember if I am thinking of my hunger?"

"Drink more water. That will help somewhat with your hunger. I know you lions get most of your fluids from your prey, but drinking water will make you feel less hungry. Also, try eating some plants. They contain fewer calories and will also fill you up. But most important is to restrict the amount of meat that you eat."

Nyack started mumbling. "First, you make me pay attention and feel things. Then I have to make pictures in my head of things. I adjusted to all that. But you want me to exercise and to eat less. Things are going very well. Why would I agree to such an outrageous suggestion?" Nyack roared.

"If you exercise and eat right, you will be even better at never forgetting. You will live longer and be able to do all the new things you are doing now. You will be able to remain king for a longer period of time. And you will be a great example to your subjects."

Nyack sighed. He walked over to a bush and pulled off a leaf. He put it in his mouth and said, "It's just not the same as a tasty zebra." With that, he walked slowly away.

I stop, and David declares, "I go to the gym four times a week and work out for an hour."

"I teach karate three times a week. I work out after my classes," Jack proclaims.

"I have to admit that I don't have time to exercise. Between the job, the house, and the kids . . ." bemoans Alice.

"I used to go to exercise classes after school, but now I help with the school play and don't have time," comments Gail.

I interrupt the barrage of remarks "I don't want you beating yourselves up about this. If you are exercising, keep it up. If not, I want to convince you to find the time to do so. The research on exercise and memory is very convincing. Let me outline a few of the studies."

1. The Salk Institute in La Jolla, California, found that adult mice that exercised on a regular basis developed twice as many new brain cells in the area that deals specifically with memory (Quartz & Sejnowski, 2002).

2. At Case Western Reserve, over 500 people were studied. Their activity levels were compared. The subjects who had been physically active were three times less likely to get Alzheimer's disease (Friedland et al., 2001).

3. According to research at Harvard Medical School, physical activity increases an important chemical in the brain called nerve growth factor. This increases the growth of new cells in the brain (McKhann & Albert, 2002).

4. Dr. Arthur Kramer at the University of Illinois tested the cognitive functioning of 124 men and women, ages sixty to seventy-five. These people rarely or never exercised. He had them either walk briskly for one hour three times per week or do yoga-type stretching. Six months later they were given a memory test, and the walkers scored 25 percent higher than those who stretched (Barlow, 2003).

"There are many other studies that support exercise. It is known to help protect your brain cells from injury. And there's also research supporting exercise and movement for students. Sifft and Khalsa [1991] reported that cross-lateral movement enhances vision, cognition, and alertness. Have I convinced you?"

The group nods, and David responds, "I already exercise, and my students do move in music class."

"I'm wondering if my students do enough exercise," Gail thinks out loud. "I may look into doing some moving with them. Cross-lateral movement . . . isn't that part of Brain Gym? One of the teachers at my school has talked about that."

"Yes. Brain Gym is a program developed by Paul and Gail Dennison [1994]. It is an excellent program that offers movement with some control. I have used it at every level that I taught. It's so nice to have some options for moving middle and high school students without the feeling of losing control. I would suggest that anyone interested check out the Web site: http://www.braingym.com. Here is a daily activity journal [see Figure 5.1] that is useful for keeping track of what you do each day. You and your students can record the amount of time you spend on each activity in the boxes. Note that climbing stairs is listed. I know some of you are up and down stairs many times throughout the school day. That counts!

"And now, the second part: Are you interested in eating right? It will make a difference in how you feel and how you think," I suggest.

"I think I eat pretty healthful foods now," John said. "I'll have some junk food occasionally, but in general, I am careful about what I eat."

"I'm not suggesting that anyone go on a diet. I think we need to talk about foods that are good for the brain. Those that appear to enhance memory. That's what this is all about. There are research studies with suggestions for better eating for our brains."

1. Academic performance improved for children participating in a national school breakfast program. They also showed fewer behavioral problems, according to research done at Massachusetts General Hospital and Harvard Medical School (Bloom, Beal, & Kupfer, 2003).

2. Research done at the Department of Psychiatry at Harvard Medical School suggests that breakfast consumption improves cognitive function related to memory, test grades, and school attendance. The elementary children who ate breakfast had 40 percent higher math grades (Alaimo, Olson, & Frongillo, 2001).

3. Eat good fat: Those foods that contain Omega-3 fats decrease the risk for cognitive decline. Foods containing Omega-3 fats include olive oil,

Figure 5.1   Fitness Journal

My Fitness Journal

Keep track of your physical activity. Try to be active every day. Record the amount of time you spent on each activity in the boxes.

Day/Date	Running	Jumping	Sports	Walking	Biking	Climbing Stairs
Monday						
Tuesday						
Wednesday						
Thursday						
Friday						
Saturday						
Sunday						

salmon, mackerel, tuna, Brazil nuts, canola oil, flaxseed oil, green leafy vegetables, and lean meats (Carper, 2000).

4. Avoid the bad fats: Omega-6 fats come from meat and other animal products. Donuts, bacon, margarine, corn oil, potato chips, steak, and processed foods fall into this category (Carper, 2000).

5. Eat fish at least twice a week. Those highest in Omega-3s are usually recommended (Small, 2002).

6. Eat food with antioxidant properties: Antioxidants help clean up the residue left from oxygen consumption in our brains. Think of what happens to a sliced apple when it is left out. It turns brown from the oxygen exposure. Think of that happening in your brain! Eat some of the following to help prevent that: raisins, blueberries, strawberries, broccoli, oranges, cherries, kiwis, onions, and corn (Small, 2002).

7. Eat five servings of fruits and vegetables each day (Small, 2002). Tomatoes contain lycopene, a strong antioxidant. In the Nun Study, Dr. Snowdon (2001) found that women in their late seventies and eighties with low blood lycopene levels showed greater cognitive problems than those with higher levels.

8. Take multivitamins. Most researchers suggest that we may not get the appropriate levels of vitamins each day from our food sources. According to Benton & Cook (1991), intelligence scores and concentration abilities of six-year-old children improve with vitamin and mineral supplements.

9. Try frozen yogurt rather than ice cream (Conyers & Wilson, 2001).

10. Be aware of your overall caloric intake. Dr. Roy Walford (2000) at UCLA found through animal studies that calorie restriction dramatically prolongs life expectancy and helps maintain optimal brain fitness.

"This is not fun. I don't want to go on a diet," Grace states. "I like to have steak occasionally."

"There's nothing wrong with an occasional steak. Or occasionally having ice cream or chips. These are suggestions for a healthier brain and a healthier life. You need to be aware of the foods that have been shown to be healthy. When you need a snack, try blueberries instead of chocolate bars. You'll probably feel better as well," I say.

In order to make this more appealing, I add, "Stand up. Let's use a mnemonic to help us remember what is healthy for our brains."

They quickly stand.

"We're going to use our bodies as a peg system to remember some healthy foods. You call out the foods and I'll help you make the connection," I offer.

"Broccoli," Alice suggests. "Isn't that a big brain food?"

"Okay, put your hand on top of your head, and instead of feeling your hair, imagine that your skull is covered in broccoli. It's cold and bumpy."

"Nuts," Jack offers.

"Take your index finger and touch your temple and say, 'Am I nuts?'"

"Blueberries," David yells out.

"Imagine your mouth is stuffed with blueberries. Now smile and picture your teeth stained blue."

"Salmon," John shouts.

"Place your hand over your heart like you're saying the pledge. But as you do, know that you are slapping a slab of salmon on your heart because salmon is good for your cardiovascular health."

"Tomatoes," Alice recommends. "For the lycopene."

"Hold out your left hand and imagine you are holding a tomato. Now squeeze it and let the juice drip down your arm."

"Yuck," Gail interjects.

"How about frozen yogurt?" Jack proposes.

"In your right hand, you are holding a scoop of frozen chocolate yogurt. Can you feel how cold it is? Oops! It's starting to melt and drip on the floor."

"Bottled water is next," Grace demands.

"While you are holding the tomato in one hand and the yogurt in the other, a wicked person walks up with a bottle of water and pours it in your pants pocket. All twelve ounces. Feel it running down your leg?"

"Sardines," Gail suggests. "I love sardines. Aren't those high in Omega-3s?"

"In your other pocket, picture sardines. Not in the can. They're swimming around in your pocket."

"Olive oil!" Ava says.

"That's easy. Sardines are packed in olive oil. So what are they swimming in inside that pocket?"

"Olive oil," they all say. "It's a greasy mess."

"Complex carbohydrates are last," Jack decides.

"Okay, look down and imagine you are standing in a field of wheat. It's grown very tall and you can't even see your feet."

"I need practice," Grace says. "Let's say it all together as Marilee shows us the body part it's attached to."

As I touch my head, temple, mouth, left hand, right hand, left pocket, right pocket, and lift my feet, they all recite the foods they chose. Everyone is impressed.

"Take a look at what you eat. Better yet, write down what you eat each day for the next week. Compare what you eat to what we've talked about . . . and next time you are at the grocery store, think about the body peg and the list we made. Maybe you'll throw a few of those things in your shopping cart! Also, have your students keep a food diary. They may be amazed at what they eat. If you model good eating habits, that may go a long way toward influencing them. I am providing you with a food journal [see Figure 5.2]. This is something both you and your students can use. Sometimes we are unaware of our actual consumption, and this provides a visual of our intake. The Harvard School of Public Health created a Healthy Eating Pyramid. It is an excellent source of information and can be found at http://www.hsph.harvard.edu/nutritionsource/pyramids.html.

"There are several areas to help you N.E.V.E.R. F.O.R.G.E.T.; this is just one of them. You each have strategies that you have used that work for you. I'm trying to give you a guide that will help you overcome any weaknesses you have. Because some of you already exercise regularly, you can concentrate on the other strategies."

"Okay, Marilee, what's the rhyme for Exercise and Eat Right?" Ava asks. "I'm going to need it because I almost never work out."

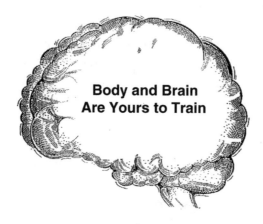

Body and Brain Are Yours to Train

"I can remember that," Gail says.

"I'm inspired. I guess the sandwich, chips, and soda I have for lunch need to be replaced. I'll stop at the grocery store on the way home," Jack mutters.

Figure 5.2   Daily Food Journal

Food Journal

Name: _____   Week of: _____

	Monday	Tuesday	Wednesday	Thursday	Friday	Saturday	Sunday
Whole Grains							
Veggies							
Fruits							
Nuts, Legumes							
Plant Oils							
Fish, Poultry, Eggs							
Dairy							
Red Meats							
Others							

MAINTAIN YOUR BRAIN

- Always check with your doctor before beginning an exercise routine. If you are not provided with specific instructions, begin with something easy, yet powerful. Walking is great exercise.
- This chapter does not suggest a diet for anyone. I am suggesting that there are foods that are known to help both body and brain. You may check to see how many of these you are eating each week. Perhaps increasing some is a possibility for you. Remember, research continues on brain foods. This list may grow or change in the future.

TRAIN THE STUDENT BRAIN

- Teach your students the body peg with the healthy foods. They will enjoy the movement, and perhaps they will share this information with their parents.
- The food pyramid has changed several times in the past few years. Put the newest one up in your room and spend some time talking about it. Even though it is not your responsibility to monitor what your students eat, it is your responsibility to help them learn. This is one way to improve performance.
- If your school or district does not provide physical education and/or recess each day, you need to add more movement in your classroom. It is well worth the few minutes it takes to get students moving.

CHAPTER SIX

R = REST

Memories Go Deep When You Get Enough Sleep

Ava	Grace	Alice	David	Jack	John	Gail	You
3	4	📖	🎵	🏀	🖼️	🔬	

Class begins with, "I can't believe how much I eat!" exclaims Alice. "Me, too," David agrees. "I kept track of my intake for two days. It's a good thing I exercise!"

"That really made me see the light," Grace acknowledges. "After just one day of keeping track, I headed to the grocery store. I walked around repeating that body peg list we made last week. I don't like sardines, but I bought everything else."

"Mnemonic devices really work well," John comments. "I use them quite often now."

"Tony, my son, and I went out to eat. It certainly is difficult to eat healthy foods at some restaurants, but we tried. I shared what we learned with Tony. He wants to start working on N.E.V.E.R. F.O.R.G.E.T. now, before he starts worrying about his memory," Ava says.

"By the way, I spoke with the nutritionist at my doctor's office and with our school nurse," David shares. "I told them both about Eating Right and gave them the list of foods. They both gave it the official okey-dokey. The nutritionist said this type of food plan would help prevent a lot of problems, including diabetes!"

"My high school students kept a food diary. They were shocked to see what and how much they consume! Some of them have three diet colas before they get to school. We talked about the nutritional value of soft drinks. I think they got the picture," Gail concludes.

"What's good for your brain is good for your body, right?" Alice asks for confirmation.

"Absolutely. There are many good books available with more nutritional information. I'll give you a list before you leave tonight. Any questions about anything we've covered in the class?"

"Marilee, I lost four pounds!" Gail says proudly. "I feel so good about myself!"

"I also lost weight," Alice announces, "and I'm feeling better."

Everyone has pretty much the same kind of comments. Exercise and eating right are beneficial.

"I have to brag," Ava begins. "I used to be a marathon runner. It was so much fun to get started again. I'm really starting to get in shape. I may even enter a race. I feel great!"

"Well, I'm never going to be Mr. Universe," comments John. "I had back trouble several years ago, so I have to be careful. But I'm walking. I go to the mall with my neighbor and we walk for an hour every weekday. My pants fit better at the waist, and the scale is starting to move. I go to school feeling very energetic."

I explain that weight loss can be a "side effect" of good exercise and eating healthy foods. Again, I suggest they see their physician about how much to exercise. Every body is different and has different requirements and restrictions.

"I am thrilled to hear how well you are doing. I know that I feel better and have a great deal of energy after working out. I have always found myself dragging when it has been more than a couple of days since I exercised."

"My principal has become involved. He's walking around the world with students at recess. They are figuring the miles to walk to go around the world. They walk around the track every day and keep a record of the distance. Some of the teachers are doing the math and others are figuring the routes. It's really an incredible journey. My students are really excited! "Let's find out about the next letter," suggests Grace. "My students are expecting it tomorrow!" what Opooit is going to have Nyack do next."

THE LION SLEEPS TONIGHT

Nyack returns to see Opooit after many weeks. It has taken him a long time to change his lifestyle. He did it slowly, as Opooit suggested.

"My, my, King Nyack!" *Opooit exclaims*, "You look young and lean."

"*I have lost a lot of weight. I think just spending more time on my feet made a big difference. I am running every day. It took the lionesses some time to get used to my new routine. I take the cubs with me for the runs. Do not worry, I have them run ahead of me so I won't lose them!*"

"*Gee, sire, you have a lot of skin hanging down from your belly. Can't you tighten that up?*"

Nyack laughs. "*That's part of being a lion, Opooit. We have skin that hangs down so we don't get hurt if we get kicked.*"

"*I am sorry, sire. I didn't know.*"

"*The running wears me out a bit. And even though I want to eat more, I find that too much food affects my exercise. This combination of factors keeps me following the rules. The rest of my time I spend exercising, noticing what goes on in my kingdom, practicing visualizing what I want to remember, and, of course, eating. Nothing like a tasty zebra for dinner! But I'm eating less of the zebra meat and adding leafy greens.*"

Opooit cringed at the thought of the zebra, but did not respond. "Well, I want you to keep that fit and trim new look, but I also want you to ponder the concept of the next letter in N.E.V.E.R."

"Yes," *Nyack replied*. "I am certainly ready for the R. I hope it doesn't take too much energy, though. I need my rest," *he declared*.

"You do need your rest; in fact, that's the next letter," *Opooit shared*.

Opooit continued, "Let's talk about that now. Along with exercise and eating right, you need rest. R is for Rest. I know you lie around, but you don't sleep enough. Sleep helps you N.E.V.E.R. F.O.R.G.E.T. Memories stay in your brain better if you sleep. What you noticed, felt, and pictured today will be stored in your brain while you sleep. So, you must continue exercising and eating right, but you must also sleep more. Decide on a plan to do all of these. Exercising more may help you sleep better. But remember, I'm not talking about the way you lie around in the shade. Get at least eight hours of sleep at night, and move around more during the day. You 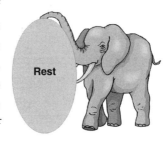 will feel better and think better. Everything else has worked so far for you. This will, too."

"How can I be considered the king of the jungle if I do not have my time to look as though I am reflecting on the needs of my kingdom? I never allow myself a deep sleep. Others will surely think I am not doing my job if I sleep a full eight hours. I will lose the respect of the other animals, and they might be afraid that I am not looking out for their interests. It is a tradition that we lions spend most of our time at the throne in order to be adored and revered. I cannot know what is happening if I am in a deep sleep."

"I know this is a difficult change for you to make, sire. But you will improve your memory if you sleep deeply. It is this sleep that will help you remember the things that you have noticed and visualized. It is sleep that will allow you to become stronger as you exercise and *eat right. It is sleep that will help you remain calm in times of adversity. Your subjects will admire a wise king who knows not only what is good for the kingdom, but also what is good for himself," Opooit declares.*

Nyack shook his head in wonderment. "I will have to give this much thought. I am not sure that I will be able to awaken from a deep sleep if danger is lurking."

Nyack walked away unhappily.

"Okay, let's talk about Rest!" John shouts excitedly. "That's an area I'm pretty good at. I sleep seven hours almost every night."

"How many of you got eight hours of sleep last night?" I ask.

No one raises his or her hand. "So, I guess you got more?"

The others laugh. Jack exclaims, "I get up at 6:00 a.m. to get to school by 6:30 a.m. for that early class. After school, I do my paperwork and my grading. I grab a bite and go to karate class or one of my kid's activities. I get them to bed by 10:00 p.m. and usually work on the house. I'm lucky if I'm in bed by midnight!"

David speaks, "I have a crazy schedule. After school I have marching band practice. Then I give private lessons. Tuesday and Thursday evenings are symphony rehearsals. I also try to create my own music. I hate to admit it, but sometimes I'm up all night when I'm on a roll! I don't think I've had eight hours sleep two nights in a row since high school."

"I don't want to get personal here, but at fifty-three, my body is going through changes. There are many nights when I fall asleep easily but wake up at 2:00 or 3:00 a.m. and can't fall back asleep," Grace shares.

The group spends several more minutes sharing their nonsleeping experiences. Then I interrupt with, "Let's look at the research and then we'll see if we can solve some of these problems. Maybe we can add some sleep for each of you.

"Again, there are many studies on sleep from very reputable institutions."

1. Dr. Robert Stickgold from Harvard University studies college students. He taught a large group a list of words. Then he let them sleep. One group he awoke after six hours sleep, and the other after eight hours. The group with eight hours sleep remembered more than the others. Stickgold and his colleagues believe that we encode, or store, our memories while we sleep. It appears that most of the encoding takes place during the last two hours of an eight-hour sleep (Stickgold, Whidbee, Schirmer, Patel, & Hobson, 2000).

2. McGill University neuroscientist Karim Nader (2003) says that memory is a process of storage and restorage. Storing a memory for long term doesn't occur all at once. It is a three-step process that relies on sleep.

3. Some studies indicate that brief naps may reverse performance declines after learning perceptual skills (Mednick et al., 2002).

4. At the University of California at San Diego, brain scans showed that sleep-deprived subjects had to work harder and recruit different parts of the brain to help with visual tasks (Bloom, Beal, & Kupfer, 2003).

5. Loss of sleep seriously affects sustained attention, cognitive speed and accuracy, working memory, reaction time, and overall behavioral capability, often without the sleep-deprived person being aware of the deficits. According to research at the University of Pennsylvania, sleep deprivation is a big problem. Sleeping only six hours at night causes a "sleep debt" that most people don't realize they have. Just missing an hour or two each night can have devastating results (Doran, Van Dongen, & Dinges, 2001).

6. One of the most recent studies dealing with school age children was conducted at Brown Medical School in Providence, Rhode Island. Seventy-four students between the ages of six and thirteen were tracked by their teachers during three weeks of varied sleep. The teachers rated the students during a normal sleep schedule, a restricted sleep schedule, and an optimized sleep schedule. When the students slept less, they were rated as more sleepy and having more problems with concentration and attention. There were also more problems with schoolwork (Fallone, Acebo, Seifer, & Carskadon, 2005).

"How many of you ever crammed for an exam?" I ask. They all raise their hands. "What happened after you took the test?"

"I forgot everything," Gail says. "I've tried to tell my students that cramming doesn't work, but they still do it."

"When you cram, you stay up late and don't get enough sleep. So cramming is a way to forget rather than a way to remember. It stores information in working memory, not long-term memory. Part of the problem is the lack of sleep time for the brain to store the learning. One of the most successful ways to increase sleep is to keep a journal. I'd like you to try keeping one for a week or two. You can also copy this and have your students try it."

"Let's talk about your students and sleep. How much sleep do they need?"

No one offers an answer.

"Research suggests that students need at least ten to twelve hours of sleep until puberty. At that time, they need nine hours and fifteen minutes [Carskadon, 1999]. If encoding new learning takes place in the last two hours of

Figure 6.1   Sleep Journal

Sleep Journal of: _____

Week of: _____

Day/Date	Time I Fell Asleep	Time I Woke Up	# of Hours of Sleep
Monday			
Tuesday			
Wednesday			
Thursday			
Friday			
Saturday			
Sunday			

a proper sleep, is it any wonder that students forget from one day to the next? I think several of you were concerned about this scenario the first night of class.

"Imagine this scenario: You have the lesson plan of the millennium. It's so good that you can't wait to teach it. It's Monday morning and all your students enter your classroom ready to learn. They've been sleeping the right amount for their age. They've been eating properly. They're excited about learning!"

"Wow!" Ava interrupts. "I've never had that happen. Not all of them."

"That's true," I continue. "This is definitely a fantasy. Anyway, they are ready to learn, and you are ready to teach this fabulous lesson. As you teach it, you can visibly see the students absorbing the information. You can practically spot the 'Aha!' moment on every face. Life seems great. After the lesson, both you and your students continue the day. They go home that evening and get varying amounts of sleep: some get nine or ten hours. Most get eight or less. The next day when they enter your room, you are ready to continue and reinforce this awesome learning; however, many of your students look at you blankly as you briefly review and continue. Even though they 'had it' yesterday, today it appears to be gone."

"Is sleep the only culprit in this scenario?" Jack asks.

"Probably not. There are many variables. The point is, sleep is important and most of your students don't realize how valuable it is. We need to reinforce this.

"At the middle and high school levels, there is an added problem with sleep. At puberty, the biological clock changes and students' sleep time shifts back an hour or so. The chemical, melatonin, that is released in the brain to help us sleep is now released an hour later, so students have trouble falling asleep. When they have to get up early for class, the melatonin is still in their brains, so they are often sleepy for the first hour of school [Carskadon, 1999]."

"So remember:

**Memories Go
Deep
When You Get
Enough Sleep**

"Sleep and exercise go together. A study at Stanford University involved forty-three people who did no regular exercise. Everyone in the group had complaints about falling asleep, waking up in the middle of the night, or waking too early. Twenty-four of the participants did thirty to forty minutes of low-impact aerobics four times a week. The rest did no exercise. Those who exercised found that after four months, their sleep improved [Goldman, Klatz, & Berger, 1999].

"Take a few minutes and talk to each other about ways to increase the amount of sleep you get. Then discuss different approaches to help your students." The group works together, and everyone forms a basic plan.

I add, "Please go slowly. As far as sleep is concerned, if you go to sleep at midnight now, don't think that you can just quickly change that to, say, ten o'clock. Go in fifteen-minute increments. Tonight, go to sleep at a quarter to twelve. Tomorrow night, try eleven-thirty. Does that make sense? And share that strategy with your students, too."

"I've wanted more sleep. I just didn't have enough reasons why. Then, when my memory started slipping, I thought I should take care of that first. I didn't know that all of this went together," John declares.

"You all know that it is fall break at the university. Therefore, we won't meet for two weeks. That will give you time to work on your new sleep routine. Continue to work on N.E.V.E.R. and have a great two weeks."

MAINTAIN YOUR BRAIN

- Americans have the habit of bragging about how little sleep they need to operate effectively. The research studies show otherwise. It is important that we model the right attitude about sleep and take better care of ourselves.
- Figure 6.2 offers sleep tips for those of all ages.

TRAIN THE STUDENT BRAIN

- Post the tips for your students. Better yet, have the students make visuals for each of the tips. Then post them in the room. Your students will be proud of their work, and the information may become more meaningful for them.
- Talk to parents at back-to-school night about the sleep research. They are the ones who need to take responsibility for their child's sleep. Show them that you will support them.

Figure 6.2   Sleep Tips

1. Don't try to sleep on a full stomach. Have a light snack at bedtime.

2. Make your room dark, cool, and quiet.

3. Keep a routine sleep time. Try to go to sleep at the same time each night.

4. Avoid foods and drinks that contain caffeine.

5. Exercise during the day. This will help make you sleepier.

6. Avoid watching television or working on the computer before bedtime. The light from these machines keeps our brains from releasing the sleep chemicals.

SOURCE: Adapted from the National Sleep Foundation (n.d.).

- Ask your students what keeps them awake at night. Some of them are experiencing stress from home or school. Have students write in their journals about their stress. Perhaps they will be willing to talk to you or someone else about their problems.

CHAPTER SEVEN

F = FREE YOURSELF OF STRESS

Lower Stress for Memory Success

Ava	Grace	Alice	David	Jack	John	Gail	You
3	4	📖	♫	🏀	(image)	🔬	

"I can't believe how much more sleep I am getting," declares Jack. "I didn't think it was possible, but that schedule you all helped me with actually works. I feel better, and I believe I have a better handle on things."

David walks in and explains, "I took the schedule home and talked it over with my wife. She convinced me to share this memory information at our monthly staff meeting. That was last week. I was adamant that they listen to this. I even looked up those studies you mentioned and made copies of them. We are forming a committee to look at our schedule. This seems so important at the middle and high school levels. It's going to be difficult, but we have decided to see if we can change our schedules. On a personal note, I have been getting about a half hour more sleep at night, and I now take a twenty-minute nap at school—during lunch. I know I'm performing better."

"The exercise seems to be helping me sleep as well," offers Grace. "The best part is that I'm starting to lose those awful bags under my eyes. I also feel much better."

The entire group agrees that more sleep helps them feel better, accomplish more, and remember more.

"I am thrilled to hear how well you are doing. I know that I feel better after a good night's sleep, and I have a great deal more energy. The undergraduate classes I teach are very early in the morning. Classes like this one and graduate classes are usually in the evening, so I know how difficult it can be to get into a good routine. But I have always found myself dragging when I cut back on sleep."

"I like what David did," interjects Gail. "I'm going to bring this information to the staff meeting next week. Parents need to be told this information and, of course, the kids, too. David, may I have copies of the studies you used?"

"I thought some of you might want them, so I made copies and brought them with me tonight," David responds. "They are pretty impressive."

"I can share them at the karate school, too," offers Jack. "We encourage self-discipline and self-esteem. I think the students and their parents can benefit from the studies. I'm sure some of the kids get little sleep. Now that I know it works for me, I'm sure I can sell others on it!"

"You know, you are all missing the boat if you aren't sharing Nyack and Opooit's story with your students. I've told them about this class and each week I share the next 'installment.' They love it. Many are telling their parents about it. I've even had a few calls. This is an opportunity to let everyone in on ways to help with learning and memory. Okay, Marilee, what's next?" asks Grace. "Let's hear what Opooit is going to have Nyack do next."

A LAID-BACK LION?

Nyack returns to see Opooit after many weeks. It has taken him a long time to change his lifestyle. He did it slowly, as Opooit suggested.

"My, my, King Nyack!" Opooit exclaims, "It is good to see you again. You are sleeping more?"

"I sleep about eight to ten hours a day. The sleep is deep and restful. There have been few emergencies and I find that one of the lionesses who is up with her cub will wake me if I do not hear someone in distress. Therefore, I do not mind the deep sleep, and actually enjoy feeling well rested. It is hard to get out of the habit of lying around on my throne most of the day."

"Do you not find all the new things you are doing take up your time?" inquired Opooit.

"Yes, they do, usually. And speaking of time, I can't stay long today. There is word that hunters are coming, and I must check with the rest of my pride and make sure they are safe. Then I must check with the subjects in my kingdom and see that they have places to hide. I must also round up all of our cubs that are probably out playing."

"Gee, it sounds like a very stressful time for you."

"It is always stressful in my line of work, or should I say lion of work?!" Nyack laughs.

Opooit smiles and says, "Let's look at this sign again. F is for Free, Free Yourself of Stress. I realize that there is some stress in everyone's life, and some stress is good. But too much stress, like you are experiencing today, is bad for your health and for your memory. Stress interferes with storing memories and retrieving memories."

Nyack looks at Opooit and back at the N.E.V.E.R. F.O.R.G.E.T. sign.

"There is no way I can be stress-free, Opooit," Nyack insisted. "I have a big job. I have to watch over my kingdom. I have to be sure that everyone is taken care of. My pride alone has thirty members. I'm sorry. This just isn't possible."

"But, sire, you are on your way to a less stressful life. By sleeping more, you are actually reducing your stress levels. Exercise does the same thing. You are in better shape than ever to take care of everything. Now you need to take a look at your life and determine what causes the most stress. Then you either change your life or you change your attitude about your life. In other words, you change your responses to some of the things you do. You choose not to get stressed."

"Is that really possible?" asks Nyack.

"It's what we elephants do to N.E.V.E.R. F.O.R.G.E.T. To free myself of stress, I ask members of my herd for help. When it is too stressful because hunters are looking for ivory, I take my herd and move to another location. Lowering my stress protects my memory. It will do the same for you. Go now, King Nyack, and see if you can free yourself of stress."

I stop. There is total silence for about thirty seconds. Then I say, "My guess is that you are examining your life to determine if stress plays a part in your memory slips. I think back to the first night of class and your stories. I knew then that stress is a problem for many of you, if not all of you. We live in a very stressful world, and the research on lowering stress is impressive. I'd like you to fill out the My Typical Day chart [see Figure 7.1]. You can choose any day of the week, or you may want to fill one out for each day of the week and take a good look at what stressors you may have in your life. Are you doing too much? Do you have any time for yourself?"

"I think I figured out what stresses me out in the mornings," Gail announces. "It's getting everyone in and out of the shower. I'll have to come up with a schedule."

"One of my stressors is my wife's family. I don't think I can change them . . . or get rid of them," adds Jack.

"Think about what Opooit told Nyack. You either change your life or you change your attitude. I have a poster up in my office. It says, 'It's not what

Figure 7.1   My Typical Day Chart

Name: _____

My Typical _____ Chart

Use this chart to write down your typical day. In the blank above, fill in the day you are working on. You may want to make a chart for each day of the week. Examine what you are doing and what possible stressors you have.

Morning	Afternoon	Evening

happens to me that counts, it's how I *respond* to what happens to me that counts.' Anyone agree with that? Can you look at your daily schedule and determine if you can change your attitude about the things you do that cause you stress? Here is a stress questionnaire [Figure 7.2]. It's called 'Are you a HAPEE person?' The letters in HAPEE stand for Healthy, Accomplished, Performing, Energetic, and Enthusiastic. These are characteristics to check on, according to the work of Dr. Bruce McEwen."

Figure 7.2   How HAPEE Are You?

Stress Research: Are You a HAPEE Person?

HAPEE is an acronym for *Healthy, Accomplished, Performing, Energized, and Enthusiastic.*

Rate yourself on the following and discover how HAPEE you are!

Good stress helps you fight disease.
Bad stress can make you sick.
On a scale of 1–10, how is your health? _____

Good stress gets you going.
Bad stress holds you back.
On a scale of 1–10, how much do you accomplish? _____

Good stress makes you smarter.
Bad stress prevents you from showing how smart you are.
On a scale of 1–10, how is your performance? _____

Good stress gives you energy.
Bad stress zaps your energy.
On a scale of 1–10, what's your energy level? _____

Good stress comes from active enthusiasm.
Bad stress can come from boredom.
On a scale of 1–10, how actively are you engaging at school or in your job? _____

Add up your score. We all want to be HAPEE every day, but sometimes we have bad days. Rate yourself over a period of two weeks. If your score is consistently below 30, it may be time to examine what stressors are in your life. You may be able to eliminate some of them or change your attitude.

SOURCE: Based on the work of McEwen & Lasley, 2002.

"After you look this over, along with your My Typical Day chart, I will share some of the stress research with you."

Several minutes pass, and the participants are ready to listen to the research.

1. People who suffer from severe stress may develop cardiovascular problems, such as a heart attack (Sapolsky, 2004).

2. Chronic stress can lower your immune system's response, making it easier for you to get colds and infections (McEwen & Lasley, 2002).

3. Stress protects under intense conditions, but chronic stress can speed up disease and cause damage to the brain (LeDoux, 2002).

4. According to the *Dana Guide to Brain Health*, in a five-year study that was published in 1998, memory tests were given to people in their seventies. They were asked to find their way through different mazes. Those who had the highest level of cortisol, a stress hormone, did worse than the others. They found that these people had also lost more brain cells in the area devoted to memory (Bloom, Beal, & Kupfer, 2003).

5. Females react differently to stress than males. The hormone oxytocin is released in the female brain during the stress response. This makes her want to talk to someone, to bond. Whereas the male experiences the fight-or-flight response, females lean toward a "tend and befriend" solution (Taylor et al., 2000). Allow your female students the opportunity to relieve stress through dialogue.

"Does that give you enough motivation to lower your stress levels? Now that you are getting more sleep, you are helping your body rid itself of some of the stress hormones it has accumulated during the day [McEwen & Lasley, 2002]. If you can possibly eliminate some of the daily stressors you encounter, you will be doing your body, your brain, and your memory a big favor."

"What about our students, Marilee? There are so many who come to school stressed. How can we help them free themselves of stress? What would you suggest?" Ava asks.

"Dr. Robert Sapolsky, the neuroscientist who wrote the book *Why Zebras Don't Get Ulcers* [2004], says that predictability, choice, a feeling of control, physical activity, and social interaction are safeguards against stress. Do you provide those for your students? Use the My Typical Day chart [Figure 7.1] and then take a look at what you are doing in the classroom in these five areas. I have a set of questions for you to use to determine if you are lowering stress." See Figure 7.3 on the next page for examples of how to lower stress in the classroom.

Figure 7.3   Examples of How You Lower Stress in the Classroom

---

How Do I Keep Stress Levels Low in My Classroom?

Use this checklist to determine why stress levels might be high in the classroom. Write down what you are currently doing. Is it working?

_____ 1. I provide predictability for my students by

_____ 2. I give my students choices in the following areas:

_____ 3. I offer my students a feeling of control by

_____ 4. I provide social interaction in the following ways:

_____ 5. I give my students the opportunity to move by

_____ 6. These are other ways I lower stress:

"I know I can offer them social interaction and physical activity. I'm not sure how much predictability I offer," Ava responds.

"I give my students predictability by always having an agenda on the board. That way, they know exactly what to expect," Gail offers.

"I think structure offers predictability; don't you think so, Marilee?" John asks.

"Both of those suggestions are good for predictability. Your classroom rules also help in this area," I reply.

"I offer my students choices. I think that gives them a feeling of control. They get to pick which assignment they do, and sometimes which topic they study," Grace chimes in.

"You are the experts in your classroom. You know your students, and you recognize most of their needs. There are situations in the course of the day that would be stressful for some. Think about those and see how you can avoid those situations. The more you can free your students of stress, the more they will remember," I suggest.

"Social interaction is very important. It's nice to have someone who will listen to your problems, especially when you are stressed about them," Alice says.

"You mean, like we do here? We're sort of a support group for each other," Gail decides.

I nod enthusiastically, "That's exactly why I keep the classes small. I want you to have each other. It's so much easier to face adversity when you know you're not in it alone. Sometimes people you like who are not terribly close to the stressful situation can be more objective. That's a thought for your classrooms. Do the students feel like they belong? Perhaps cooperative-learning groups would offer some of them a feeling of bonding with the other students.

"I use a poster [see Figure 7.4] and some 'stress strips' with my K–8 students [see Figure 7.5]. First, we look at and discuss the poster. I then have these strips for them to grab as they enter the room. They can choose whichever 'feels' right to them. They can leave them on their desks and as I wander around the room, I can get an idea of how high the stress levels might be. They enjoy the faces, and although some students don't take one, it is an option for them.

"I would like you to take your charts, and during the next week see if you can identify some of those stressors. Now, some of us do things that are stressful, but the stress is somewhat invigorating. That is considered good stress. Keep doing the positive things you've been doing: Notice, Emote, Visualize, Exercise, and Rest. Opooit would be proud of you!"

"Wait, everybody, she hasn't given us our rhyme to help us remember!" David exclaims.

Figure 7.4   Feelings: How Are You Feeling Today?

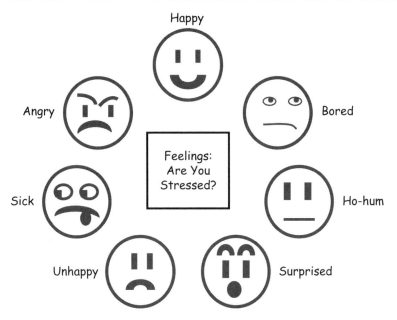

Instruct students to take a bookmark as they enter
the room and place them on their desks.

Figure 7.5   Stress Strips

Today I feel	Today I feel	Today I feel	Today I feel	Today I feel	Today I feel	Today I feel
😊	😲	😐	😐	☹️	🤢	😠
because...	because...	because...	because...	because...	because...	because...

These strips may be used for students to identify how they are feeling each day.
These categories are areas that may be associated with stress levels.

They all look at me. "See, your memory is getting better all the time, David!" I joke. "Okay, here it is:

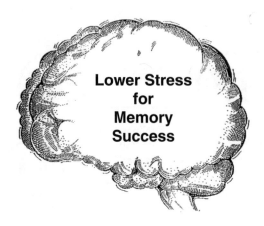

"Have a stressless week!"

MAINTAIN YOUR BRAIN

- Stress can lower your immune system. Examine the stressors in your life and see what you can do to change them or change your response to them. Fill out the chart that my class completed and see what you think.
- Meditation, exercise, and sleep are all stress relievers. If you are following the N.E.V.E.R. F.O.R.G.E.T. program, you are on your way to lowering your stress. Check out the research; it may inspire you to continue with the plan.

TRAIN THE STUDENT BRAIN

- Discuss possible stress sources with your students. Have them fill out the typical day charts. Brainstorm ways to deal with social issues, bullying, and high-stakes test pressure.
- Do you provide what Dr. Sapolsky says are important for controlling stress? Fill out the checklist in Figure 7.3 (see Page 73) every four to six weeks to be sure you are providing these for your students.

CHAPTER EIGHT

O = ORGANIZATION

Put Information in Its Place
for a Strong Memory Trace

Ava	Grace	Alice	David	Jack	John	Gail	You
3	4	📖	♫	🏀	👤	🔬	

It is five minutes after the hour and class has begun. I am talking about stress.

Alice dashes into the room and interrupts.

"I am so sorry I'm late. I couldn't find my keys. The kids wouldn't clean up after dinner, and I had to run the dishwasher. The phone rang and it was some telemarketer. My husband always tells me to hang up on them, but I just can't do that. Anyway, when I finally found my keys, I forgot where I had put my purse. I got into the car and there was no gas, so I had to stop at the gas station," Alice blurts this all out in one breath.

"It looks like you are the poster child for stress!" John suggests. "We were supposed to take this week to free ourselves of stress."

Alice takes a deep breath. "You're right. And I did. Sort of. It's my kids. I was always at home taking care of everything, and now they won't do anything to help me. They're thirteen and fifteen. I guess old habits are hard to break."

"But if they're causing you stress, you need to do something about it," David declares. "Or I guess you can change your response . . . just don't let it bother you that they aren't helpful."

"Better yet," offers Grace, "don't do the things that they won't do. Let the dishes and laundry pile up. Do yours, but not theirs. Let them see that it's time they were more independent. But you really have to not let the piles stress you more. You have to change your response to that."

"It sounds like we have some stress reduction experts here. While Alice is thinking about all of these pieces of advice, let's hear about your week. How did everyone do?" I ask.

"I made some changes in my classroom. I started making things 'predictable.' The students and I created a set of classroom rules with consequences if they were broken. It was very interesting. Some of my hard-to-handle students got involved. I thought they might want to make the list easy, but since they got to be a part of this, they suggested some tough consequences. And so far, everyone is following the rules," Grace explains.

She continues, "I really believe that since I am noticing more, that is, paying better attention to what my students need, they are responding more and paying more attention, too. I continue to share Opooit's story with them. They are fascinated!"

"I just do too much," offers Jack. "You all heard my schedule last week. I thought about it and decided to cut out two of my karate classes. That gives me time to get the work done around the house. I really keyed in on what you said last week about physical activity and stress. Even though I teach P.E., I find that many of my students would rather sit on the bleachers and not participate. After noticing them for a few days, I realized that these kids are more stressed than the others. So, I'm starting off each day with some calisthenics. Everyone has to participate."

"Well, I started meditating," announces Gail. "I learned how to meditate in college. I did it for a while in my younger days of teaching, and it really did help. I decided last week when I left, and I started the next morning. I meditate twice a day for about twenty minutes. I am much better at changing my response to what happens."

"There's wonderful research on meditation, Gail. That's something we all should be doing. Meditation lowers heart rate and releases stress hormones [Ratey, 2001]. I'm glad it's working so well for you. Anyone else want to share? How about you, David?" I ask.

"When I started sleeping more, I think I lowered my stress. But last week got me thinking. I have several stressors throughout my week, so I'm going to tackle them one at a time. The first is the way the scheduling is done for my classes. I spoke with the counselors and the principal, and I will be involved more in working out the schedule starting next semester. Also, when my students enter the music room, they just sort of do their own thing. I added a specific routine that they follow each day. I think they like knowing what to do!" David answered.

John begins with, "Dealing with middle schoolers is a real challenge. You know, hormones and such? Well, I have started working on giving them choices. I think they do feel more in control. Instead of not doing what I ask, they pick something to do and do it! It has really changed the atmosphere of my classroom!"

"I remember my middle school teaching days, John," I respond. "I had a very tough time initially. I did some reading on stress, the brain, and adolescents. Because the part of the brain that controls emotion, the prefrontal cortex, is so underdeveloped, these students have trouble with decisions. But they also want autonomy [Feinstein, 2004]. Keep us informed!"

All eyes turn to Alice. "Well," she begins, "I really am not always as stressed as I appeared when I arrived tonight. I am working on stress . . . getting rid of it, not getting it! I started delegating work at the library. I always thought that I had to do everything, but I don't. Things will get done without me as long as others know what their responsibility is. Some of the aides even thanked me. They were kind of bored because I was doing all the work. So, I'm getting less stressed. I've also started turning over more responsibility to the students. They are loving it. Do you think it's related to stress relief?"

"I think they are getting a feeling of control and perhaps some predictability since they now know what to do," I suggest.

"Why can't you do the same thing with your own kids? Maybe they need something to do to feel useful," proposes Jack.

"I hadn't thought about that. Maybe I should treat home like work. I shouldn't have to do everything. Thanks, Jack," Alice says appreciatively.

"Can we take a few minutes to look at our papers from last week?" asks Ava. "I found it very helpful to look at the whole week and found stressors on some days and none on others. For instance, I value time with my parents, but it is difficult to manage work, family, and finding time to see them. I don't know how much longer they'll be around. So, I figured out that they can help me with some of my schoolwork. They were delighted when I asked them."

"Great idea!" Grace declares. "I value my health, and I really think I'm doing a better job with that since I started making time for exercise and more sleep."

Gail breaks in with, "I think exercise is important, too, and now I'm making time for it. It's interesting how many of our stressors are related to time."

"Time management issues often cause stress. That's why we need to prioritize what we value," I offer.

"I have to admit that my stress is high because I value money. There are lots of things I want. But in order to get them, I have to work longer hours and spend my weekends away from the family giving private lessons. That's when I find the most stress. I've decided to change my priorities," David says.

"I'm using this chart with my students. It's interesting to see how logical they are when they look at the whole week. Most of them recognized their stressors! With their permission, I may share this with the parents at conference time," Ava states.

"I hadn't thought about doing this with the kids, but I just may try it. Can we get to the story, Marilee?" John requests.

"Before we get back to our story, perhaps this would be a good time for a little self-assessment. I want to know how comfortable you are with the strategies so far. This is sort of my midcourse report card. I have a self-assessment sheet for you to fill out. It will only take a few minutes, and it will give you time to reflect on what we've done," I say as I pass out the papers.

"I just want you to look at each strategy and decide whether you feel you are still at the beginning stage, in which you need reminders about the strategy; at the developing stage, in which you don't need reminders but you need practice; or at the secure stage, in which you have it mastered. Any questions?"

"I'm impressed with myself because I can remember what the acronym stands for . . . at least what we've learned so far. And I can also remember the rhymes. This is definitely good material," Ava comments.

"I don't know that I feel secure in any of these, but I do feel as if I'm developing in every area. I came here an exercise buff, so maybe I'm secure in that," says David.

"I want to take this home and think about it," Grace declares.

"As long as you feel you are ready to continue with tonight's episode. I don't want to bog you down with more strategies if you're not ready," I respond.

The group states that they are ready and want to add the next strategy to the assessment. Next week they will discuss where they are on the continuum of beginning, developing, and secure stages in their memory abilities.

"I can't show up at school tomorrow without the next saga of Opooit and Nyack!" Grace exclaims.

Figure 8.1 Assessment of Strategies

Strategy	Mnemonic Rhyme	Beginning	Developing	Secure
Notice	Intention increases retention			
Emotion	Emotion is the potion			
Visualize	A picture in your mind creates a memory you can find			
Exercise	Body and brain are yours to train			
Rest	Memories go deep when you get enough sleep			
Free	Lower stress for memory success			

NYACK LEARNS TO SORT THINGS OUT

If you've never heard a king whistling as he strolls along the riverbank, it's a sound that is really music to most subjects' ears. The whole kingdom was relaxing because Nyack became calmer. The animals still came to ask Opooit questions about things they had forgotten, but now they were more relaxed and shared their excitement about the change of pace in the land.

Opooit was quite surprised and pleased. He went to find Nyack, since Nyack had not visited him in several weeks. He thought Nyack had given up, so he was very curious to hear how the transformation had actually come about. He found Nyack at the river whistling his happy tune.

"King Nyack," Opooit called. "You seem to be very happy."

"Oh, Opooit," Nyack answered. "I am so relaxed. Life is grrreat! I thought about what you said, and at first, I was just going to skip the F in N.E.V.E.R. F.O.R.G.E.T. But then I thought

about how successful I have been with the other suggestions, so I tried to figure out how to free myself of stress. I took a trip north to see my father, King Nyack I. He is retired and living on an animal reserve. He couldn't believe how good I looked.

"I told him about my meetings with you. At first, he thought I was mad to be listening to an elephant. No offense, Opooit. He's old-fashioned, but he couldn't discount how well things were going for me. I rattled off the things I could remember, and he was very impressed. Then I talked with him about this stress thing. He admitted that he had been under a lot of stress himself when he was king. He said he believed that he retired early just to get away from all the negativity. Subjects were always afraid and angry. He noticed them going to the elephants but never bothered to find out why. He just constantly roamed his kingdom, and even when he would lie down those twenty-one hours a day, he never really slept much. That convinced me I did not want to live my life like that, so I asked him what I could do. He said, 'To get here to see me, you have traveled far from your kingdom and will be gone for several days. It will take another day for you to get back. When you return, see how things are. If you have been a good leader, everything will be okay, and perhaps you don't need to worry so much. If something is amiss, then know that you must get better in that area and train someone to take care of it when you are busy. Assign responsibility to one of your subjects.' I thought that was a genius idea. I came home and everything was fine. Knowing that I am becoming a better leader took a lot of stress off me. I am so happy that I did forget to come see you. I guess I need more help with my memory!"

Opooit and Nyack both laughed. Opooit picked up a stick with his trunk and by the side of the river scratched out N.E.V.E.R. F.O.R.G.E.T. Next to the O, he wrote Organize.

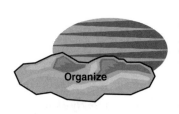

"This is a very important part of never forgetting. If you organize your thoughts, your memories, and yourself, you will remember much more. For instance, you have taken it upon yourself to notice where your subjects hide their food. That information can be put in a category called Food Hideaways. That will help you never forget them and let you find that information faster."

"Are you saying that I can take these memories and arrange them differently to help in never forgetting them?"

"Yes. Once you have a place in your memory for hideaways, when you see a new one, you add it to that category."

"I rather like Organize, Opooit. I think it will relieve more stress. I will practice organizing my memories and get back to you." With that, Nyack continued his stroll on the riverbank whistling a happy tune.

"We have done some visual organization through our visualization strategy. Your brain likes to organize information, but it doesn't tell you how it has done so. Therefore, you need to be actively involved in that organization. Imagine two students who have identical materials in their desks. One is very organized and has each item in a specific spot. The other just throws things in there. You ask them to take out a pen or protractor. Who is going to find the item faster? How you organize can make accessing memories easier. Some possible ways to organize include classification, sequencing, cause and effect, and compare/contrast. Each of these takes information and puts it into a pattern in your brain. The rhyming peg system is a way of organizing information to make it easier to remember.

"If I ask you to remember the following list, what strategy could you use to organize it?"

- Pear
- Robe
- Tire
- Apple
- Shirt
- Orange
- Speedometer
- Headlight
- Dress

"Well, there are three possible categories: fruit, clothing, and car parts," offers Alice.

"Good. How many of you know your driver's license number? No one. We don't need to give that information often enough to commit it to memory. How about your social security number? All of you. How do you remember it?" I ask.

"Well, I chunked it into three numbers. Like we do with phone numbers," Grace says.

"Exactly. Chunking is a strategy that organizes information into larger chunks to help us remember. When you first learn a seven-digit phone number, you repeat it over and over again. You can only hold seven chunks of information in your immediate memory [Gamon & Bragdon, 2001]. Then, as you get to know it, you chunk it into two bits of information—the first three numerals and then the last four. Look at these letters and try to remember them:

ciafbijfkusanbc

"Once I remove them from your vision, you have trouble remembering them. But if I organize them into chunks like this—cia fbi jfk usa nbc—they become larger chunks and you know exactly what they are!"

"Jack, how do you organize the equipment in the gym?" I inquire.

"Well, I do it by categories. The volleyball equipment is in one locker, the basketball equipment in another, and so on. I could put all the balls together, but that would not be as efficient. This way, the kids get everything they need from one spot," Jack finishes.

"So, there are some ways of organization that are better than others," I state. "How do you remember a movie?"

"Movies are stories, so they have a beginning, a middle, and an end," Alice says. "So you remember them in that order."

"Could we organize memories in story form?" I ask.

David now speaks, "That's what people do with their dreams. They really only have bits and pieces of what they dreamed, but when they retell the dream, they often make it into a story."

"So we *could* organize information by putting it into a story and make it easier to remember!" Ava exclaims.

"What about acronyms and acrostics? Are they organizational strategies? I use those to teach my students," Gail explains.

I nod, and John asks, "What are acronyms and acrostics?"

"Acronyms are like the letters in N.E.V.E.R. F.O.R.G.E.T. They each represent a word or phrase. Acrostics are sentences you make up in which the first letter stands for something. An example is Every Good Boy Does Fine, which identifies the lines from top to bottom in a treble clef [Sprenger, 1999]," I clarify.

"If I organize my life, will I be able to remember better?" asks Alice.

"The more organized you are, that is, the more procedures you follow, the easier it will be to handle things. For instance, you couldn't find your keys. Do you have a spot where you always keep them?" I ask.

Alice nods.

"Except when you don't, right?" Everyone laughs, having experienced the same thing. "So, you had to retrace your steps until you found them. That's why organization is helpful. You save time and aggravation.

"Think of all this as a giant filing system. If you want to remember something, arrange it in a way that you can find it. This strategy will help your students as well. They need to learn how to organize their notes, materials, and their brains! Here is a sheet of mnemonic devices you may want to try."

Figure 8.2   Mnemonics

Method	*Example*
Acrostic: an invented sentence in which the first letter of each word is a cue to an idea you need to remember.	ROY G. BIV: Red, Orange, Yellow, Green, Blue, Indigo, Violet (colors of the rainbow)
Acronym: an invented combination of letters with each letter acting as a cue to an idea you need to remember.	Every Good Boy Does Fine: E,G,B,D,F (Notes on a treble clef)
Method of loci: Imagine placing the items you want to remember in specific locations in a room with which you are familiar (this is sometimes called a memory map).	Kitchen: stove, oven, microwave, refrigerator, sink, coffee pot, toaster, window, trash can, telephone
Chaining: Constructing a story that contains each element of a list.	South America married North America in Europe and they had four children whose names all begin with A: Asia, Africa, Antarctica, and Australia
Image name: Associating something about the person to remember their name.	Shirley Temple has curly hair (curly Shirley)
Music: Putting information to a melody and singing it.	My students sang their prepositions to popular songs
Rhyming peg: Associating a word on concept to the item associated with the number. One must first memorize the key words in the peg: One is the sun Six are sticks Two is a shoe Seven is heaven Three is a tree Eight is gate Four is a door Nine is line Five is a hive Ten is hen	To remember a grocery list—broccoli, milk, eggs, and so on—one might first think of the sun and have broccoli hanging from the sunrays; since two is shoe, one's shoes might be milk cartons; eggs might be imagined growing on trees; and so on
Spelling mnemonics: These are often acronyms.	Big Elephants Can Always Understand Small Elephants: BECAUSE
Rhymes	*i* before e except after *c*, and *weird* is just weird!

"Your mnemonic for this is

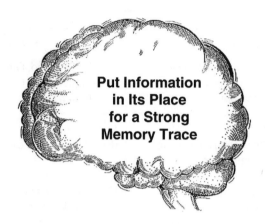

**Put Information
in Its Place
for a Strong
Memory Trace**

"In other words, arrange information so you'll be able to access it easily. See you next week, and don't forget the assessment."

MAINTAIN YOUR BRAIN

- If you are like me, your desk is stacked with papers—but you know where everything is. Sometimes it works that way with our brains, and sometimes it doesn't. Because memory is so malleable, it is important to create ways of remembering. Think about areas in your life that are troublesome and need organization. Set some goals to organize those areas.
- Fill in the chart that the class participants took home with them. If you are sharing this information with others, make copies and have them also fill it out. Determine where you think you are in the N.E.V.E.R. F.O.R.G.E.T. course.
- Keeping a list of mnemonic devices handy at your desk or in your plan book may be helpful (see Figure 8.2).

TRAIN THE STUDENT BRAIN

- Teaching your students to sort information into categories is one way for them to see how it can be organized. If they create the categories themselves, that will be a higher level of thinking (Marzano, Pickering, & Pollack, 2001).

- Homework is difficult for many students to organize. Be sure all assignments are in visual form on the chalkboard or the overhead before they leave for the day.
- Your room will run more smoothly if the students are familiar with organizational procedures. Spend the first week of the school year repeating your procedures. Keep in mind that student brains are not fully developed; therefore, repetition is a must!

CHAPTER NINE

R = REHEARSE

Rehearsal's a Way to Help Memories Stay

Ava	Grace	Alice	David	Jack	John	Gail	You
3	4	📖	🎵	🏀	🖼️	🔬	

"We met for dinner before class to talk about the assessment," Alice announces when class begins. "We thought about asking you to join us, but we wanted a chance to talk about the strategies openly."

"So you *are* becoming your own support group. That's great. And meeting is a nice organizational skill. Did you come to some conclusions?" I ask.

"We all feel that we're doing well. The class is easing our minds and taking us down the road we were looking for. We find that our strengths are different. Just as our needs are. As a group, we feel we are all developing in most areas. A few of us are secure in some areas, but we feel we need more practice," John reveals. "We made a composite assessment for you."

"That sounds very fair. I'm glad you took the opportunity to get together. I hope I didn't miss a fabulous meal," I joke. "How did you do with organization?"

"I'm a visual learner," Gail says. "I found myself going back to the mind-mapping idea. They help me organize a lot of my lessons."

"I have a story to share," John announces. "I did some research on the compare/contrast idea. I learned that if students can identify similarities and differences, they can raise their standardized test scores as much as 45 percent

Figure 9.1   Assessment of Strategies

Strategy	Mnemonic Rhyme	Beginning	Developing	Secure
Notice	Intention increases retention		All	
Emotion	Emotion is the potion		All	
Visualize	A picture in your mind creates a memory you can find		All	
Exercise	Body and brain are yours to train		Alice, Gail Grace, John, Ava	David, Jack
Rest	Memories go deep when you get enough sleep		All	
Free	Lower stress for memory success	Alice	Gail, Grace, John, Ava, Jack, David	
Organize	Put information in its place for a strong memory trace	All		

[Marzano, Pickering, & Pollack, 2001]. So I started using the Venn diagram with them. I gave them an assignment in which they had to compare two of the short stories we had read this quarter. I modeled this by comparing and contrasting short stories and novels. I am still working on personal involvement and emotion. But I was very concerned about organization with students at this level. I thought of last week and the organizational skills. Do you all know a Venn diagram? It's two circles overlapping. I put "short story" in the large part of the left circle and "novel" in the right. Where the two circles overlapped, I listed their similarities. Under each name, I listed their differences. When I finished with the diagram, I knew just what to say. I, too, am a very visual learner, and I could remember the information that the diagram depicted."

Figure 9.2   Venn Diagram to Help Organize Information for Memory

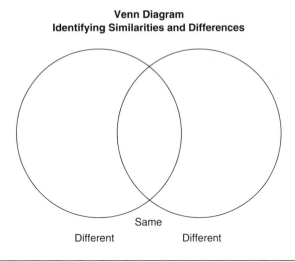

Figure 9.3   Venn Diagram Comparing Short Story and Novel

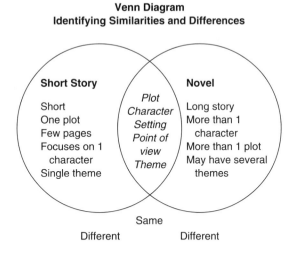

"Good organizational tool, John. For those of you who are unfamiliar with a Venn diagram, I'll draw one for you," I offer.

"Will you show us what yours looked like, John?" Gail asks.

"This reinforces our study of the elements of the short story as well," John comments as he finishes his diagram.

"Research has shown that organizing information helps put it in long-term memory. At Toronto University, students were given one hundred cards with one hundred different words on them. Some students were told to memorize the words; the others were told to categorize them. Both groups remembered the words equally well. That's pretty impressive, isn't it?" I ask.

"I organized using a few of our strategies," says Ava. "We are reading *Sarah Plain and Tall*. I started by having the students read and create lists of words describing Maine and the prairie. They wrote them in their Reader Response Journals. Then I gave them a copy of a Venn diagram. They created their diagrams after I modeled one for them. They liked using them. In another chapter of the book, I worked on organizing information by cause and effect as well as sequencing. We talked about sequences showing the order of events in a story or passage, and that cause-and-effect relationships identify events in the story and why they happen. For the sequencing section, I had the students use a stair-step graphic organizer [see Figure 9.4]. On the first step, they wrote the first thing that happened, and so on. For the cause and effect, I simply used a T chart [see Figure 9.5]. On the left they listed causes, and on the right they listed effects. I think we are all enjoying using graphic organizers."

Figure 9.4   Graphic Organizer for Sequencing Events in a Story

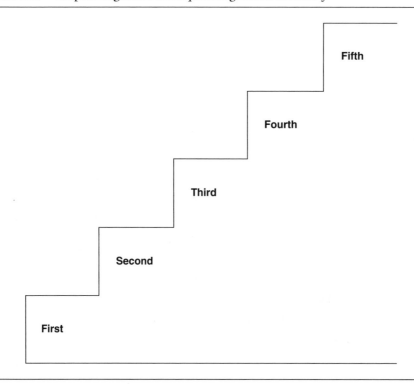

Figure 9.5   T Chart Graphic Organizer for Cause and Effect

Cause	Effect

"There's also strong research about the effectiveness of graphic organizers [Marzano, Pickering, & Pollack, 2001]," I share.

David interrupts, "I tried something different. I had a list of things to do and parents to see, so I created a story. It was like I saw myself completing each thing on the list. It was fascinating. I pictured myself conferencing with each parent. Then I saw myself leave school and go to the music store to pick up some music for one of the selections we'll be working on. I left the music store and headed home for some private lessons in my basement. It was like I was watching myself on television. Everything went pretty smoothly. We finished the conferences early, and my wife asked me to meet her for coffee to talk about it. Have I mentioned that she is also a music teacher? I had time, so we met. Then I just backtracked in my mind and knew what I had to do next. I really liked organizing my day that way."

"I really like that idea," Alice comments. "I'm going to give that one a try. I took my kids a 'to do' list and categorized what I wanted done. I gave them each a category and wouldn't let them watch television or play outside until they finished. It worked well."

I beam as I listen to each participant's success story. It is always so fascinating to hear how different organizational strategies work for different individuals.

"I put three new paper holders on my desk. One is marked Urgent, next is Must Do, and the last is Might Do. I think they're going to help me keep track of what is important. I'm ready to hear how Nyack did with organization, and I want to know what the *R* word is," Grace speaks up. "Is everyone else ready?"

PRACTICE WHAT YOU PREACH

Exactly one week later, Nyack showed up at Opooit's place. He still whistled as he walked.

As soon as Opooit saw him, he stopped what he was doing and said, "Hello, sire, you seem very happy today."

"I am a happy king today, Opooit. I have organized my memories, and they are strong." With that, he gave a gentle roar. "I am trying to learn and remember information about my kingdom and subjects. I am using categories. For instance, there are four types of animals in my kingdom that are endangered. They are the white and black rhinoceroses, the pygmy hippopotamus, the mountain zebra, and, as much as I hate to say this, my friend, the elephant."

"It is sad to be so vulnerable," Opooit said, nodding.

"Another category I have made is endangered animals in Africa that are not in my kingdom. They include the mountain gorilla, leopard, and cheetah. I will continue to categorize and otherwise organize material that, as king, I should have at my fingertips.

"I still know where the food hideaways are, and I am attempting to classify the four seasons according to what predators may be stalking my subjects."

Opooit raised his trunk and trumpeted. He couldn't help himself; he was so excited for Nyack. "King, you are doing an excellent job. It won't be long before everyone will be coming to you for answers instead of me!"

"Will that make you sad, Opooit? I do not wish to hurt you in any way."

"Oh, no, sire, it is all I can do to keep up with my herd. I will cherish the extra time I will have," Opooit lied. He knew he would miss the company and the questions, but he still didn't want to be king!

Nyack walked over to the N.E.V.E.R. F.O.R.G.E.T. sign. "What's R?" he demanded.

"R is for Rehearse. You have learned many strategies for never forgetting. Rehearsal is the means by which you practice what you learn. An example is the categories you just mentioned. *If you rehearse them, they will stay in your long-term memory and be easier to use when you need them. Rehearsal can include practicing in different ways to help you never forget. When I rehearse some categories, I sometimes sing them to help me remember. That is a form of rehearsal. I am sure to get my sleep in between my practice sessions since I know that helps get the memory solidly embedded in my brain."*

"R is for Rehearse, eh? I can do that. I will rehearse and make sure I know the answers to the questions that my subjects ask. I will rehearse at night, before I go to sleep. I will practice until I am perfect! Thank you, Opooit." And he walked away, still whistling.

"Practice makes permanent. In other words, before you rehearse, make sure you are rehearsing exactly what you want to remember. Practice it wrong, and it will take about three weeks to get the damage undone. Rehearsal can be either rote or elaborate [Sprenger, 2003]. Rote rehearsal is simply repeating something over and over. Most of the research says this doesn't work well. We probably all learned our multiplication tables that way, and, I don't know about you, but I still remember mine! Elaborative rehearsal involves some of the techniques we are using: visualization, emotion, and organization. Once we have elaborated on the material, we do need some repetition to make it stick. Here are some rehearsal pointers:

- Rehearse one topic in multiple ways: reorganize (Marzano, Pickering, & Pollack, 2001)

  If you have learned the information with a visual mnemonic, like the rhyming peg, you may want to categorize it or put it to music. This second memory system will help you retrieve the information faster or under different circumstances.

- Overlearn: learn past perfection (Schenck, 2000)

  When you think you have learned something perfectly, keep rehearsing. Once the brain makes the right connection for your memory, it needs to reinforce that connection until it becomes automatic. Think of how you learned to ride a bike. At first it took great effort, but the more you practiced, the more it became second nature.

- Make time to sleep in between rehearsals: don't cram

  We have talked about the importance of sleep. This is a reminder that cramming doesn't work well. It's really a way to forget rather than a way to remember. It takes sleep time to get our memories fully encoded in our brains.

- Rehearse in the place where you will present the information (Baddeley, 1999)

   Research has shown that people who learn something underwater—yes, underwater—remember it better underwater! This location memory that David experienced by going into his office where he designed the school performance proves how powerful our surroundings can be. These are memory triggers. Use them if you are able.

- Take breaks during rehearsal time

   Your brains are not designed for nonstop learning. Take breaks when you are rehearsing. This is called the "spacing effect" and has been shown to be effective! Your brain can only focus on one kind of sensory stimulation for about twenty minutes. Your students' focus time is their age in minutes (DeFina, 2003). Once that focus time ends, you must change the type of stimuli coming into the brain.

I stop here and check for understanding. "Do those pointers make sense to you?"

"So, if I use an acronym, I should also use something else?" asks Gail.

"That's what you've modeled here," Grace states matter-of-factly. "We have N.E.V.E.R. F.O.R.G.E.T., and we have your rhymes. That's why we all remember what we've learned!"

At this, they all nod in agreement. I hear comments like, "No wonder this is working" and "I'm definitely going to use this reorganize pointer."

"Here's your rehearsal rhyme. I hope you like it."

"I am going to suggest to you that you reorganize some of the learning you have been doing recently. If you used a mind map or categories, for instance, see

Rehearsal's a
Way
to Make
Memories Stay

if you can rehearse the material in another way. I realize that some of you don't have information that must be memorized for the long term; you are more concerned with immediate memories. But practicing this technique will help you remember it when you need it. This will really help your students as well. See you all next week!"

MAINTAIN YOUR BRAIN

- Challenge your brain to remember. When you need groceries, write down the list, and then see if you can use a rehearsal strategy to remember it without looking at the list at the store.
- Create a family tree. See how important associations are as you make it. For instance, if I am creating a list for a family reunion, I may think of a cousin who I associate with her husband and children, and so on.

TRAIN THE STUDENT BRAIN

- Educational research suggests that new learning may take more than twenty-four rehearsals (Marzano, Pickering, & Pollack, 2001). Vary the rehearsal strategies that you use with your students. Try to notice which rehearsal works best for each student.
- Encourage your students to get enough sleep for memory storage. If they study a few minutes each night, information has a better chance of becoming long-term memories. Remind them that going over their notes counts as a rehearsal!

CHAPTER TEN

G = GUARD YOUR BRAIN

Avoid Some Pain and Protect Your Brain!

Ava	Grace	Alice	David	Jack	John	Gail	You
3	4	📖	🎵	🏀		🔬	

"When I was in school studying music, the orchestra pit was sometimes the classroom. We sat or stood in our places learning new things. That was a way of reorganizing the material and giving us greater access. Wouldn't that be right, Marilee?" David asks.

"There are several different memory systems in the brain. When you study from a textbook, lecture, or video, you are using the semantic system. It involves words. When your instructors had you standing in the orchestra pit or an exam room, they were getting information into episodic memory, the location, plus they were using procedural memory. Procedural memory is sometimes called muscle memory. You use it when you drive a car. This is memory that becomes nonconscious. You don't realize that you're accessing the memory. It is a very powerful system, and some researchers believe that it is more reliable and longer lasting than semantic memory [Sprenger, 2005]," I finish.

"So, can I rehearse in all three of those systems?" Ava asks.

"Yes. Many of you probably did just that. As I said, the semantic system is through words or text. So, if you are studying for a driver's test, you probably start out by learning the rules in the book. That's semantic. When you practice in the car, you are using procedural memory. That's in your muscles when you learn it well. If you are used to practicing in a particular car, episodic memory, the location helps out. Does that make sense?" I study their faces for confirmation.

"That means that if I study the music, I am using semantic memory. When I practice in the classroom, I am using episodic for the location and also procedural," David announces.

"And when I learn about equipment, rules, and plays, I'm using semantic memory. When I practice in the gym, I'm using episodic memory. And the movements access procedural memory, too!" Jack says with confidence.

"How many of you have walked into a room and wondered why you were there?" I ask.

Everyone nods and a few moan. "It's so frustrating and embarrassing," Gail says.

"It was experiences like that, along with missing appointments, that sent me into memory research," I explain. "Here is one of my scenarios. I am sitting at the kitchen table reading the newspaper. I turn to the book section and, upon reading the book titles, remember that I have a book due at the library. I stand up and head for my bedroom where the book is on my nightstand. I get five steps out of the kitchen and wonder what in the world I am doing! I stop and think. But that doesn't work."

Alice interrupts, "That's a short-term memory glitch."

"Yes it is," I agree. "But now what do I do? I go back to the kitchen and look around. I am hoping to find a memory trigger. I am looking in episodic memory. If that doesn't work, I go back to the table to continue what I was doing. I am back in the same spot and the same position. Procedural memory. When I look down at the newspaper, what do I see?"

"The books again. You remember!" Grace and John say in unison.

"You're right. So we automatically use these strong systems in a nonconscious way. What I'm hoping rehearsal will teach you is that you can use them consciously to help your memories."

"What about singing?" Gail asks.

"Singing information is great for memory," I reply. "Are you using that with your students?"

"I feel that I have to know things like the periodic table, so I put that kind of material to music to help myself. Then I offer it to the students. It really works well."

"Music and rhymes are wonderful rehearsal strategies. They are ways of elaborating or expanding on the information. You're using a system that will hold the information indefinitely," I explain. "Let me give you a little quiz. Finish these statements:

- Winston tastes good . . . "like a cigarette should!" they all say together.
- My baloney has a first name, it's . . . "O-S-C-A-R," they sing back.
- Nothin' says lovin' . . . "like something from the oven!" they laugh as they sing.

"Why do you remember this trivia?" I pose the question.

"Rhythm, rhyme, and music," several say.

"Your brain loves it. So why not use it as a way to expand your memory and the memories of your students? It's a great reorganization and rehearsal tool. The more we store information in different ways in our brains, the easier it will be to recall it. Most of the time, as adults, we don't have a lot of information to memorize. For that reason, we don't practice our strategies. When it comes time to use them, we're a bit rusty."

"Because of what they say about the brain—use it or lose it?" Jack wants to know.

"Exactly. We may still be able to recall our old strategies, but it takes some time. Have you ever taken a class or professional development workshop and found it difficult to 'get into the groove' of learning and studying?" I raise the question.

"Oh, yes," Grace responds. "I have to go for professional development and learn all kinds of information based on the 'latest and the greatest.' I feel like a kid—not a very bright one, either!"

"Well, now I feel as if I can remember anything. The tools we are getting from you, and, of course, from Opooit, are really helping me. It will be a matter of keeping it up after class ends," Gail says. "I'll probably have the easiest time of it, though. I'm teaching all this to my students, so it's getting reinforced all the time. Some of my weaker students have commented to me about how they are really looking over the material each night before bed and having a much better memory of what we are learning."

Ava wants to know, "Is there a Memory 102?"

They all laugh.

"I have a rehearsal question," Alice announces. "I took some information that I had visualized using the method of location. I used my living room at home. Then, for rehearsal, besides going over the visuals I had from that method, I tried categorizing. They both worked, but I still feel the visual is the best way for me to go. Should I only use visual strategies?"

"I believe, and have taught all my students, that it is always wise to stretch. Reorganizing your material and rehearsing in different modes will help you keep the dissimilar strategies strong in your mind. They will be more accessible to you when you need them. Start with your strength—the visual approach— because you want to be sure that you do learn and remember, but then try something different for practice. Because a different approach may be more difficult for you, you will only be concentrating on the strategy since you already know the content. Does that make sense?"

There is no further discussion, so I get into my storytelling mode. I bring out my bicycle helmet that is shaped like a brain and put it on before I begin.

"That's kind of gross," John remarks. "My middle school students would love it!"

"I thought this might be a good way to prepare you for the next letter," I respond.

"*G* is for Gross?" Jack laughs.

And so I begin.

NYACK'S ON GUARD

Opooit was taking a walk on a sunny afternoon and heard a roar. He believed it sounded like Nyack, and he wondered if everything was okay. As he continued walking, he heard another,

milder roar, and he began to hear Nyack's voice. Opooit followed the sounds to a clearing, where Nyack was standing on a rock speaking. There was no one around. Opooit was concerned that Nyack had really lost his mind.

"King Nyack, are you all right?"

Nyack looked up, a bit surprised. "Of course I'm all right, Opooit. I'm just doing what you said. I'm rehearsing."

"What are you rehearsing, sire?"

"I'm rehearsing my speech. When I complete the N.E.V.E.R. F.O.R.G.E.T. program with you, I am going to share my marvelous memory with my subjects. I must let them know that I am able to answer their questions. So, I am rehearsing my speech and all the bits of information they will want. I have categorized everything in my memory, and now I am visualizing the information on the rocks, bushes, and trees out here. It is working quite well."

"I am sorry I interrupted you," Opooit said sincerely.

"Oh, that's fine. I was about to finish and come to see you. I am eager for the G. You know, Opooit, this is like a mystery to be solved. The mystery of N.E.V.E.R. F.O.R.G.E.T. and the mystery of my memory. Come now, what does G stand for?"

"*G is for Guard Your Brain,*" *Opooit said with conviction.*

"*Why do I need to guard my brain? It seems silly,*" *Nyack responded.*

"*Oh, no, sire, it is not silly at all. After all, you are responsible for making important decisions that affect the lives of so many creatures, great and small! Your brain must be protected!*" *Opooit declared.*

"*I guess if I had a head injury, I could forget all the wonderful things you have taught me. I would also not be much use to my subjects. If I will have the ability to tell them where to find food, when to hide, and how the weather is going to be, I'd better have my wits about me. I remember a previous king who had been shot by a hunter. The bullet went into his brain. It was amazing that he did not die. The lionesses took care of him and he remained on the throne. But after a short period of time, he could no longer rule the kingdom. He was confused and he slept most of the time.*"

"*So, he was replaced?*" *asked Opooit.*

"*Yes, by my uncle,*" *replied Nyack.* "*It was very sad to see a king end his reign like that. You are so very right, Opooit. I must guard my brain. I will have other creatures as my bodyguards. They will walk with me when the hunters are close by, and they shall shield my head at all costs.*"

"*That is an excellent idea, sire,*" *Opooit said sincerely.*

With that, Nyack left the elephant and walked quickly back to his lair. He looked both ways as he walked in case there were hunters around.

"What do you think?" I ask with interest.

"I think this is huge," Jack replied. "I am constantly bombarded by parents who worry about their children playing sports. It's so important that they wear their equipment!"

"There has been some research on soccer," Alice blurts out. "There's not much equipment for that sport. Kids should not be 'heading' the ball when they play. I read a study that said it affects their cognitive abilities."

"I think we have to look beyond sports," Grace remarks. "There are parents who don't insist that their kids wear seatbelts! It doesn't seem to matter that it's a law. How can they be so foolish when it comes to their kids' brains?"

"What about the bike riders, skateboarders, and inline skaters? Shouldn't they be wearing protection?" asks Ava.

"Hey, I've had kids conk themselves on the head with their tubas! There's danger everywhere!" David jokes.

"Aren't there other ways to guard your brain? What about drugs and alcohol? Can't those be damaging to our brains? And what about our students who use and abuse these substances?" asks Grace.

"Wow!" says Gail. "We've got a lot more bullets to dodge than old Nyack has!"

"While you are thinking of scenarios where we must be better protected . . . and I did say we. After all, we are all in danger of head trauma, and Gail is right, there are other ways we must guard our brains. Let me offer some research on the subject," I interject.

- According to Paul Blanton, director of the University of Alabama at Birmingham's Sports-Related Concussion Program, the biggest mistake parents and coaches make is in determining whether a student has a concussion. A child may not lose consciousness and still may have serious problems.
- Injuries due to falls from playground equipment result in a higher proportion of severe injuries than either bicycle or motor vehicle crashes, according to a new Children's Hospital Medical Center of Cincinnati study of emergency department visits throughout the United States (Children's Hospital Medical Center of Cincinnati, 2001).
- Over one million Americans are treated and released from hospital emergency departments as a result of traumatic brain injury; an estimated fifty thousand die from such injuries each year. Physical, cognitive, behavioral, or emotional impairments, either transient or permanent, can be caused by traumatic brain injury. They range from subtle to severe and can result in seizure disorders (Liotta, 2004).
- According to the 2002 Monitoring the Future survey, roughly 30 percent of twelfth graders reported drinking five or more drinks in a row in the two weeks before being surveyed (Johnston, O'Malley, & Bachman, 2003).
- Helmets are essential in football, baseball, ice hockey, skiing, in-line skating, skateboarding, scootering, and snowboarding (Harvard Medical School, 2005).
- After brain trauma, there may be persistent emotional and/or cognitive disabilities that include short-term memory loss, long-term memory loss, a slowing down of the ability to process information, trouble paying attention, problems finding words, and difficulty multitasking (Bloom, Beal, & Kupfer, 2003).

"Whoa, stop there. What are we going to do about preventing this?" David asks.

"Let's make a list of ways to guard our brains [see Figure 10.1 on page 106] and those of our students," Gail suggests.

I give them a large sheet of poster paper, and they begin. The discussion continues about seatbelts, and then they talk about helmets—for bikes, football, skateboards, and skates. No drugs or alcohol. Limit caffeine and sugar intake. Limit television and violent video games.

"Wow, the list looks great. Can anyone think of anything else?" I ask.

Ava responds with, "I think we should state everything in the positive."

"That's a great point. Some of the research suggests that the brain responds to nouns and verbs first. Then it looks at negatives. So, 'Don't spill your milk' may be recognized by the brain as 'Spill your milk!' Let's tell everyone what we *want* them to do," I add.

"What's the mnemonic for this one?" David asks. "I think that should head the list."

"Well, that will be a great title. I can't wait to put this up in my classroom. It's going to start some interesting discussions," Gail decides.

"I think I'll send it home to the parents with the weekly newsletter. With my young students, the parents are pretty good at reading what I send home," Ava adds.

"And I'll be sure to put it up in the gym," says Jack. "There are sometimes accidents in P.E. class, and I'm always concerned about head injuries in particular."

"It's time to go. I'd like to add one more suggestion to get your students involved in this concept. Try a slogan like 'Are you insane? Guard your brain!' Ask students to create posters that fall under this heading. They could draw kids abusing alcohol or drugs, smoking, or playing sports without a helmet. It will depend on the age level as to which direction you may want to go. Let them be creative. Have a great week!

Figure 10.1   List of Ways to Guard Your Brain

Avoid Some Pain: Protect Your Brain!

- Always wear a helmet for football, motorcycling, bicycling, skating, skateboarding, etc.

- Avoid "heading" a soccer ball.

- Wear your seatbelt.

- Hang out with others who avoid alcohol and drugs.

- Spend time with positive people.

- Limit the amount of television you watch.

- Avoid violent video games.

- Eat brain-smart food.

- Exercise regularly.

- Avoid smoking.

- Look both ways before crossing a street.

- Take care on playground equipment.

- Look before you leap: Make sure you are diving in safe waters!

MAINTAIN YOUR BRAIN

- Be careful around chemicals. Preventingharm.org is a Web site with the latest neurotoxins listed. The organization is dedicated to keeping individuals out of harm's way. Visit the Web site.
- Mild traumatic brain injury is a health problem. Be aware that mild concussions can cause behavioral problems over time. Be careful on ladders and doing common household tasks. Alzheimer's is a concern we all have. Head injury has been linked to the disease.

TRAIN THE STUDENT BRAIN

- Make parents aware of the possible consequences of head injury.
- Information on the effects of drugs and alcohol should be available at your school. Check with the counseling department and ask for a presentation for your students. Dr. Daniel Amen has a DVD called "Which Brain Do You Want?" It covers the effects of alcohol and drugs. It's available at http://amenclinics.com/store/product_info.php?products_id=81&osCsi d=8f702ab9dfc8972b88420b0cf8ddbb8c
- Begin a campaign titled "Avoid Some Pain: Guard Your Brain!" Have students create pictures of different ways to protect their brains.
- Remind students to be careful on the playground before and after school, during recess, and during P.E. class.
- Helmets do not prevent accidents, but they can lower the effects of injury by as much as 85 percent. Encourage your students to not only wear helmets when riding their bikes, but also to be careful to avoid collisions.

CHAPTER ELEVEN

E = ENRICH YOUR BRAIN

New Directions Create New Connections

Ava	Grace	Alice	David	Jack	John	Gail	You
3	4						

"It's hard to believe we only have one more class!" exclaims Gail. "It's gone so fast!"

"It's gone quickly for me, too," Jack responds. "And I feel like I've accomplished a lot!"

"I just started a campaign against drugs and alcohol," Gail states. "It's the 'Save Your Brain Campaign'! And I think it's going to work."

"I like the sound of that. Maybe we can get things going at the middle school, too," John responds. "I also want to work on kids wearing helmets when they are on their dirt bikes and three wheelers."

"A student in my class shared the story of his cousin who fell off his skateboard and had a head injury. My students were mesmerized by the account. The child had a concussion and had many difficulties for months thereafter. I think my students began to take Guard Your Brain very seriously," Grace volunteers. "As you suggested to us, Marilee, I had one of my budding artists draw a picture of a boy falling off his skateboard and landing on his head. The caption is 'Are you insane? Protect your brain . . . wear a helmet!'"

"We had our coaches' meeting on Tuesday. I shared the information and statistics with them. We are going to try to get the professional development director to bring in a speaker on head injuries at our next district inservice. Many coaches know the dangers, but we have new coaches who need the information, and we could all use an update," Jack comments.

"I'm having the students make N.E.V.E.R. F.O.R.G.E.T. posters for the library. It's been fun and informative for them. One of my students drew an elephant with a helmet on his head and his big ears sticking out. It's so cute!" Alice exclaimed.

"I'm so glad this concept is being utilized. It's an area that we don't often discuss with our students, and it's so important!" I exclaim. "Are you ready for the next episode?"

Everyone nods and I begin.

NYACK TRIES SOMETHING NEW

Nyack entered the clearing where Opooit made his home. There were two younger lions by his side. When he saw Opooit, he turned to his companions and said, "You two stay here and keep guard."

"How do you like my bodyguards, Opooit?" Nyack asked. "They are with me to guard me and my brain. It actually relieves some stress for me."

Opooit nodded approvingly. "I am glad you are taking Guard Your Brain seriously."

"Of course, I must!" Nyack replied. "My brain is getting better and better. My memories are clear. I do not want to take any chances of injuring my brain!"

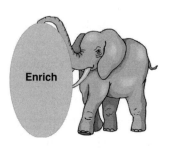

"I have my cubs guarded as well," he continued. "After all, one of them will replace me as king someday. I want their brains to be the best that they can be!"

"Now, Opooit, I think I am ready for the E in F.O.R.G.E.T."

"E is for Enrich Your Brain," Opooit says with conviction.

"Enrich my brain? How in the world am I supposed to enrich my brain? I'm up to my mane with running a kingdom. What can I possibly do that I'm not already doing?" Nyack sounded disturbed.

Opooit tried to explain, "Enriching your brain means you interact with new creatures, you take some risks, and you challenge yourself. This is an opportunity to use your brain and your memory in different capacities. Running a kingdom is wonderful, and you are doing an *excellent job, but you are not using all the brain and memory power that you have. It is time to expand your horizons. Get to know some other animals better. Interact with them. Share your memories with new friends. Make new memories with old friends. Try some new and different things. Sing. Dance. Play a musical instrument. Garden. Travel. All these activities will challenge you and make you stronger."*

Nyack liked the word stronger. "If I start enriching my brain, then my memory will get stronger?"

"Elephants never forget because they enrich their brains. Their brains are always busy with new memories as well as old ones. Enrichment allows you the opportunity to have others be part of your memory. And if you ever need help remembering, they will be around to help you. Enriching your brain will help you N.E.V.E.R. F.O.R.G.E.T."

"Very well, Opooit, I shall find ways to enrich my brain. I must do it in a kingly manner, of course. So this may take some time. I will contact you when I have discovered ways to enrich my brain. Now I must continue to rehearse my speech. I am not used to giving speeches. Perhaps I am already enriching my brain by trying public speaking..."

"This was not what I expected," David says abruptly. "I don't have time to do anything else."

"Let me give you some information about his point," I offer. "If we want our brains to stay active, we need to enrich them. We want to make as many connections in our brains as we can. That way, through injury or aging or disease, we will be able to afford to lose a few of those connections [Bloom, Beal, & Kupfer, 2003]. But I want to add that everything you have done so far in this class has been enrichment for your brain.

"Have any of you read about the Nun Study?" I ask.

"I read about it. Some nuns in Minnesota live to be really old. A neuroscientist studies their brains when they die to find out why they show few signs of dementia or Alzheimer's disease. Right?" Alice inquires.

"Yes, that's the gist of it. Dr. David Snowdon [2001] discovered these women who age well. He has found through his studies that because they remain so mentally active, when they do get dementia or Alzheimer's, they don't show the symptoms as readily. In other words, they have spare connections and the problems take longer to show. These women are active. They play Jeopardy, read, play bridge, garden, and some teach. In their nineties, they are involved in these activities. They are challenging their brains."

"Well, that sounds convincing," David admits.

"Of course, it could be that these women are living so long and are mentally active because they were never married or had kids!" Alice jokes.

They chuckle at that thought, but quickly they are back on track.

"So, do we get involved in the types of things Opooit mentioned?" Jack wonders.

"Anything that works for you. You teach karate. That's physical. How about taking bridge lessons? According to Dr. Marian Diamond [2002] of the University of California at Berkeley, bridge is one of the best enrichment activities for your brain," I explain.

"I played bridge years ago. Maybe I'll try it again," Jack responds.

"Here's a chart you can take home with you and fill in if you feel it will help. I created the categories based on previous classes. I know enriching your brain doesn't happen overnight . . . or even in a week. But think of ways you can get involved. Share your memories with others and create new ones."

"And the rhyme is . . . ?" Grace wants to know.

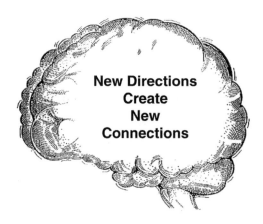

"Get involved in something new and keep your brain young and vital. Only you can make it happen. New connections will also allow you to take more new directions. It's an important step. Any questions?" I ask.

"Is this going to help our students?" Ava wants to know.

"I think it's important that they have different things going on in their lives," Jack declares.

"But some of the kids are so overprogrammed," Gail says. "Will we be pushing them too hard?"

"Perhaps the best way for you to approach Enrich Your Brain [Figure 11.1] with them is to tell them that the more involved they are in their classroom activities, the more connections they will make in their brains. It will be easier to access information if there are many routes to it," I suggest.

"There is also a concept called 'testing at your threshold' [Roizen & Oz, 2005]. This involves finding what your competency level is on any topic and

Figure 11.1   Enrich Your Brain Chart

Things I've Always Wanted to Try	People I Want to Get to Know	Places I'd Like to Go	Volunteer Work I'd Like to Do

pushing yourself. In other words, discovering at what level a student is in algebra and offering problems just a step above. This creates new brain growth.

"Research also shows that the higher your education is, the better off your brain will be. You will be stretching your brain capacity. Make sense?" I ask.

"I read that a common tip is to change your routine," Grace announces. "Change your route to work, the order in which you do things, and probably the way you teach a subject."

"New Directions Make New Connections. I like it. I just wonder if I can do it," David whispers to himself as they all leave.

MAINTAIN YOUR BRAIN

- Meet new and interesting people by taking an academic class, starting a book group, joining an organization, or attending more social events.
- Challenge your brain by working crossword puzzles, learning to play bridge or chess, learning a new language, or taking music lessons.
- Access and use different parts of your brain by doing something you haven't done before. If you are interested in gardening but have never done it, give it a try!

TRAIN THE STUDENT BRAIN

- Enrichment in the classroom involves contrast. Create an environment that is different than the one the students have elsewhere. This could involve taking field trips, offering projects or subjects that they've never had, or having them work together to do problem-based or project-based learning.
- Challenge your students' brains with logic problems, lateral thinking puzzles, and thought-provoking questions.
- Keep students thinking. Try to add "What else?" or "Tell me more" in response to their answers.

CHAPTER TWELVE

T=TEACH

*Share What You Know
and Feel Memories Grow*

Ava	Grace	Alice	David	Jack	John	Gail	You
3	4	📖	🎵	🏀		🔬	

"I can't believe it's the last night of class. It's really been fun getting to know everyone," Gail announces as I walk in.

"It's difficult for me, too," Ava responds. "It's like we've bonded here. Sharing our problems and all."

"You all know my secrets," Jack says with a grin.

"Are you available for motivational talks, Marilee? I'd love to have you come and speak to the entire school. There are so many educators with similar problems. Stress levels are so high," Grace declares.

"I'd love to come. Just give me a call. You all have my contact information."

"So, you're available for phone pep talks when I forget something?" Jack asks.

"Well, I'm not the psychic hotline, but if you need some reassurance, give me a call."

"My son, Tony, and I started volunteering," Ava shares. "It was great. We went to the Mission on Saturday and prepared and served lunches. It made us both feel good, and I think it's a great way to make some new connections."

"I have always wanted to be in a rock band," John declares. "To enrich my brain, I bought a guitar. When I become famous, you can say you knew me 'when.' Actually, you can all say you helped me become a star!"

"My wife and I called the old bridge group. We are meeting in two weeks to begin playing again," Jack states. "I've also started working the Sunday cross-word puzzle."

"I've changed my after-school routine. I still work out, but I changed the time. Dinner is earlier, and I tried brushing my teeth with my nondominant hand. It was weird!" Grace says.

"Gail and I are going to take cooking classes together," Alice announces. "We were talking on our way out to the parking lot last week and discovered that we don't cook as much as we would like. So, we're going to the kitchen shop at the mall where they offer classes in the evenings."

"I think we should all be invited over to your homes for dinner . . . after you take the lessons. After all, if it weren't for this class, you probably wouldn't be doing this!" Jack exclaims.

Alice jumps in with, "And I'm challenging all of the students who come into the library. We have the Accelerated Reader program. It's where the kids pick books and take a computerized test on them. I am challenging them to read books that are just a little bit harder—just above their comfort level. I talked to the teachers and we've looked at test results to determine as closely as possible their reading levels. The students are responding well to the challenge. I've made a chart with their names. It's titled 'Enrichment Makes Brains Grow: Stretching Their Reading Brains [Figure 12.1].' I have little brains that I move across the chart. I don't have their reading levels listed, so no one knows. It just shows progress. I brought a sample to show you.

"Some of the teachers are using the chart in their classrooms. Not for Accelerated Reader, for other reading activities. I think it's great!"

Ava and Grace look at each other. Almost in unison they say, "I might just copy that, if you don't mind."

"I want to hear what happens with our two friends, Nyack and Opooit," John states. "Time is passing, and since this is the last class . . ."

"I almost hate to have it end," Jack admits.

"It's time, isn't it?"

Everyone gets comfortable and awaits the final installment of the story.

Figure 12.1   Enrichment Chart for Reading

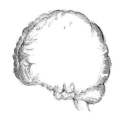

**Enrichment Makes Brains Grow:
Stretching Their Reading Brains**

Each time students challenge their reading, their brain moves to the next letter of STRETCH.

Reading Growth = Brain Growth	S	T	R	E	T	C	H
Adams, Billy	🧠						
Brown, Amy	🧠						
Gingrich, Joey		🧠					
Jones, Sherry			🧠				
Smith, Alex		🧠					

THE TEACHER KING

There were several animals waiting in line to talk to Opooit. They all needed answers to important questions because their memories were so poor. He had just finished speaking to a warthog, and he noticed the animal scurried away quickly. Opooit thought there might be a predator close by. As he finished that thought, a lioness approached him. "Well," he thought, "that explains the frightened warthog!"

"Opooit," the lioness began, "I need to talk to you. I want to know what you have done to my husband. He is behaving so differently. At first, I thought he had lost his mind. Then I thought he was going through a second childhood—all that running with the cubs. Now, he's spending more time with me and the other females. And I must admit, I do like his company. He's so organized. And he can tell me where I put things! He's talking about taking us on some trips, and he's been whistling! Is this just a spell you have him under? He says he's learning from you—will all of this stick? Or is he going to change back to that lump that lies around for twenty-one hours a day?"

Opooit smiled. "Your Highness, I am sorry that the changes you see caused you any concern. Your husband is working hard to become a better king. A side effect of this is that he is becoming a more compassionate creature. At this time, he is trying to get involved with things that make him happy. You are one of those. I do believe that the changes you see are permanent. But there is no way of knowing that for sure. He is very dedicated, so we can hope that this new lifestyle will remain. Have I answered your questions?"

"Can you tell me what the secret is?" she whispered. "I would love to know and change a few others."

"At this time, Your Highness, I feel I must wait to discuss this with the king. I believe the secret may be his alone to share."

"Thank you, Opooit, for what you have done. My family and the entire pride appreciate it." With that, she walked away with a smile.

A short while later, Nyack arrived. He was ready to deliver his first speech. He had rehearsed. He had his memories organized. Some were categorical, some were cause and effect, and his speech was structured with the location of the event. Each tree and bush had been associated with a visual representation of what he was going to say. He knew he would impress his subjects.

Before he could call his kingdom to the clearing to listen to him, he knew he must see Opooit and find out what the last letter in the acronym stands for. He wanted to make sure he would N.E.V.E.R. F.O.R.G.E.T.

As soon as he spotted Opooit, he began, "I am eating a variety of food now. It is difficult. The lionesses do not understand how I can turn down some of their kill, but they are getting accustomed to many new characteristics. I am ready to become the king I want to be. But I must know about the T. I want to be sure that I have all the keys to never forgetting."

Opooit nodded. "Yes, sire, you need to know about the T. It stands for Teach."

Teach

"I am going to teach," Nyack said. "A good king is also a good teacher."

"That is true, sire. This step is to help you see that what you have done thus far are all steps that you can share. We all remember better what we teach. Sometimes, when we are in stressful situations, we revert back to our old ways. The T is to remind you that the more you share with others, the more you will also remember."

"Opooit, I thank you from the bottom of my heart. I can wear my crown proudly now. I am going to call my subjects to the clearing and introduce them to the new king.

"Will you come?"

"I will be proud to," Opooit replied.

"And, Opooit, I have come to a decision. I will continue to N.E.V.E.R. F.O.R.G.E.T. so I can help my kingdom. But I would also like you to teach my entire kingdom the secret to N.E.V.E.R. F.O.R.G.E.T. I know I wanted to be the clever one with all the answers, but I believe the kingdom will run much better if each animal is able to be more independent. I will know what they need to know, so I can help. If we all know how to N.E.V.E.R. F.O.R.G.E.T., there will be less stress in the kingdom. There will be healthier subjects who eat right and sleep better. They will know how to visualize, free themselves of stress, and rehearse and organize what they want to know, and they will be able to enrich their brains and feel emotion to make great memories. I guess what I am saying is that they, too, can take control and teach each other."

"This is why you are king," Opooit began earnestly. "I was only willing to give the animals answers. I thought that was teaching. You are willing to give them the tools they need to find their own answers. I will teach them. I would be honored if you would help me. There are so many subjects in your kingdom, and you are such a fine example of how it is possible to N.E.V.E.R. F.O.R.G.E.T., even if you are not an elephant!"

Nyack smiled. The two walked to the clearing to call the animals and begin the speech.

"Wow! It's 'give a man a fish and he eats for a day; teach a man to fish and he eats for a lifetime.' Pretty impressive," David utters.

"Most of us have started teaching this information," Alice states.

"Like Opooit said, we will learn more when we teach," I say.

"You have all started to take control of your lives by following the N.E.V.E.R. F.O.R.G.E.T. method. You have been practicing the principles for several weeks. But as Opooit said, when push comes to shove—when you are no longer coming to this class—and something happens that would ordinarily cause you to go back to your old routine, you have to remember the principles.

The more you teach this information, the easier it will be to stick with it and continue to

- Notice what is going on
- Emote to strengthen your memories
- Visualize what you need to know
- Exercise and eat right
- Rest more
- Free yourself of stress
- Organize what you need to do and what you need to know
- Rehearse
- Guard your brain
- Enrich yourself by challenging your brain

"So, teaching will keep us on track. Teach it once and learn it twice?" asks John.

"It's taking charge of our lives, so we can hang on to our memories," Grace states.

"It's also knowing that sometimes you need to write things down. Some people carry their short-term memories in a notebook. I don't think that will happen to any of you to any great extent. But it is okay to write things down. I use sticky notes. My motto is, Some memories stick better with glue!" I say.

"It's 'Walk the talk and talk the walk!' What's our mnemonic for Teach?" Gail asks.

"Share what I know and memories will grow," Alice personalizes it. "I'll remember that. I'll remember all of you. This has been such a wonderful experience. I think everyone should take this class."

"Nyack has the right idea. I'm going to see if I can get the school district to have you as the keynote speaker for our opening day next year. Everyone needs this information. It would be heavenly to lower the stress at school," Gail says wistfully. "And then, after you speak, I will continue to teach this information."

"I want to give you the Memory Questionnaire that you took the second week of class. It's a bit different as I added some questions to see if you can apply what we've learned [Figure 12.2]. See how you do, and see if you can figure out why you might have been having some trouble," I suggest.

"Wow! Most of the problems on this deal with attention," says Jack.

"No, I think it's more organizational," Ava suggests.

"I think you've really helped me," Grace states. "And looking at the student questionnaire, I can see how to help my students now."

"Before you go, we need to have a graduation ceremony," I announce.

I turn on the CD player and play the song "Memories" from the *Cats* production and call each participant up to receive the graduation certificate [Figure 12.3].

After the ceremony, I make an announcement. "I will miss seeing you, but I have a reunion each year for all the people in my classes. It will be next fall. If you want to attend for some reinforcement or just to catch up with everyone, I will send you each an invitation."

"Cool," Jack says.

"That's a great idea! See you all next fall," Grace says. There are a few hugs. They say their goodbyes and leave.

As I pack up my things, I wonder who will show up next year at the reunion and how they will have done with the strategies. And I laugh to myself as I wonder if I will remember everyone's name! I can only hope . . . and hang on to their registrations and pictures so I can practice!

MAINTAIN YOUR BRAIN

- No one has to tell a teacher how the act of teaching strengthens learning in the classroom. Be sure to apply this principle elsewhere for yourself. For instance, as you acquire new hardware, software, or other electronic materials, after you are taught how to use it, teach someone else. It will help the process become more automatic for you.

- With aging parents, ask them to tell you how to do something. An example might be asking your mother how to bake a pie or your father how to fix a toilet. Not only will you learn something, but also you will give them the opportunity to share information that they may not have retrieved in a long time.

Figure 12.2   Final Memory Questionnaire for Adults

Final Questionnaire: What's Your Memory Quotient?

1. I forget names of people right after I am introduced to them. Why? What can I do?

2. I sometimes miss appointments. Why? What can I do?

3. I forget where I put my keys. Why? What can I do?

4. I forget where I park my car in a large parking lot. Why? What can I do?

5. I sometimes have trouble finding words when I speak. Why? What can I do?

6. I occasionally forget important dates like birthdays. Why? What can I do?

7. I forget what someone just told me. Why? What can I do?

8. I forget directions. Why? What can I do?

9. I forget what I read. Why? What can I do?

10. I forget what I was just saying. Why? What can I do?

Figure 12.3   Graduation Certificate

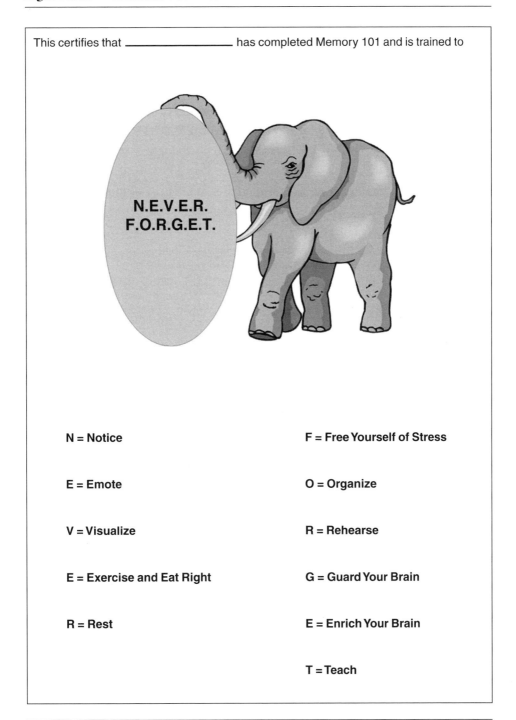

This certifies that _____ has completed Memory 101 and is trained to

N.E.V.E.R.
F.O.R.G.E.T.

N = Notice	**F = Free Yourself of Stress**
E = Emote	**O = Organize**
V = Visualize	**R = Rehearse**
E = Exercise and Eat Right	**G = Guard Your Brain**
R = Rest	**E = Enrich Your Brain**
	T = Teach

TRAIN THE STUDENT BRAIN

- As you lecture, pause and ask your students to "think, pair, share." That is, ask them to think about the material you've given, pair up, and share their understanding. This will allow them to target any questions they have.
- Reciprocal teaching is an activity that also offers students the opportunity to teach. It takes place in the form of a dialogue between teachers and students regarding sections of text. The dialogue is structured by the use of four strategies: summarizing, question generating, clarifying, and predicting. The teacher and students take turns assuming the role of teacher in leading this dialogue (Palinscar & Brown, 1985).

CHAPTER THIRTEEN

THE REUNION

Ava	Grace	Alice	David	Jack	John	Gail	You
3	4	📖	🎵	🏀	🖼️	🔬	

I am putting the finishing touches on some decorations. I have reserved the faculty lounge on the fourth floor of University Hall. The food table is loaded with brain food: bottles of water, blueberries, broccoli, nuts, tomatoes, bananas, sardines in olive oil, and a tub of ice with pint containers of frozen yogurt. The plates and napkins have elephants on them. The song "Memories Are Made of This," sung by Dean Martin, is playing in the background.

I look at the list of people who called to RSVP. There were five Memory 101 classes last year, and most of the participants are coming to the reunion. I hope they are coming to celebrate.

People start arriving. The night before, I took a quick look through last year's participant folders to make sure I knew everyone's name. I did and was pleased with myself.

Suddenly we hear music coming from the hallway. Before I get a chance to look, John steps in playing his guitar. He is playing, "I Remember You." I laugh and hug both him and his guitar.

"You stuck with it, John," I say excitedly. "This is wonderful!"

"Everything has gone really well since the class, Marilee. I'm working out almost every day. I still take guitar lessons. And I'm thinking about getting a band together!"

Just at that moment, David arrives. He has a suitcase in hand.

"David, good to see you. Are you planning on moving in?" John asks.

"I guess no one knows," David begins. "I've moved. I came back for the reunion. I just flew in and took a cab over here. I was offered the job of director of music for a much larger school district in Chicago. The responsibility is greater, but so is the salary. In the big city, I can really get to more symphonies."

He turns to me, "I owe this all to you. My confidence soared after this class. I got more involved and I had no more memory problems at work. In fact, it was quite the opposite. Things got so organized and the strategies helped the kids so much that we won a state competition; that's how I was 'discovered' by my new district. They came to visit, and this was too good to pass up. Thanks."

"I think you only have yourself to thank, David. You put forth the effort," I comment sincerely.

"Hey, everybody, what's going on?" It is Gail with Alice right behind her.

"We were just talking about David's new job in Chicago. How are you two doing?" I ask.

"I'm doing very well," Alice replies. "Where's Jack? I have to tell him that I finally got my kids on board with helping me out. Oh, there he is. Jack, come on over here."

Jack joins them as Gail shares her year. "Well, Alice and I are still taking cooking classes. It's a nice break from teaching. I opened our school year with a memory presentation. It was great. I think everyone decided to follow at least some of the suggestions. We even call each other 'Opooit' when we remember something!"

I mingle with participants from other classes as the group continues catching up.

"I am doing great," Jack says. "My schedule is more like a normal person's. I can actually get eight hours sleep some nights! I still get stressed at work once in a while, but I use that location system in my office to help me remember."

"Are you still playing bridge, Jack?" Graces asks as I walk over.

"Bridge isn't really my game. We play occasionally, though. I've become the coach of my daughter's chess team, and this past spring, I planted a garden with my wife and kids. Brain food: tomatoes and a few other veggies. I find that gardening really relaxes me. How about you, Grace?"

"For the first time ever, I'm taking the time to travel. I'm trying to make some new connections that way. By the way, I shared some Memory 101 information with the staff. Everyone really enjoyed it, and I think it's made a difference. Say, is Ava here yet?"

"She'll be here soon. How's your memory, John?" Gail quickly changes the subject.

John strums his guitar. "My memory is great. I'm using more music in the classroom and it is really helping my students remember, too. I bring my guitar in and we make up little songs for some of the information they need to know."

Figure 13.1 The Words Represented by N.E.V.E.R. F.O.R.G.E.T. and the Mnemonics

Notice	Intention Increases Retention
Emote	Emotion Is the Potion
Visualize	A Picture in Your Mind Creates a Memory You Can Find
Exercise and Eat Right	Body and Brain Are Yours to Train
Rest	Memories Go Deep When You Get Enough Sleep
Free Yourself of Stress	Lower Stress for Memory Success
Organize	Put Information in Its Place for a Strong Memory Trace
Rehearse	Rehearsal's a Way to Make Memories Stay
Guard Your Brain	Avoid Some Pain and Protect Your Brain
Enrich Your Brain	New Directions Create New Connections
Teach	Share What You Know and Feel Memories Grow

"Hey, everybody," David shouts. "Let's see if we remember the mnemonics Marilee gave us for each letter of N.E.V.E.R. F.O.R.G.E.T. Ready? All together now."

They complete the rhymes and give themselves a round of applause.

I ask for the group's attention. Before I can get any words out of my mouth, Ava walks through the door. She is carrying the largest stuffed elephant I have ever seen.

"Sorry I'm so late, everyone. My friend here kept wanting to stop and eat bushes."

Everyone laughs.

"Marilee, we all wanted to do something special for you. Gail and I called your secretary to get the names and numbers of everyone here tonight. We all pitched in and bought you the biggest elephant we could find. We all so appreciate learning to N.E.V.E.R. F.O.R.G.E.T., so we thought that if we gave you an 'Opooit' this size that you would never forget us!" Ava beamed. "He represents how much our memories have grown."

I blush and get teary-eyed. "I don't know how to thank you. I want to say that I'll never forget any of you, but we all know better. It was a great year, and I'm happy that so many of you feel successful in this memory challenge that we all face. Thank you all for coming."

"We think Opooit and Nyack belong in a book, so others can benefit from their story," Grace suggests.

"We want to be in it, too!" adds Alice.

The crowd says their good-byes. I pack up the leftovers and start thinking, "A book . . . I guess Opooit's story does need to be shared."

REFERENCES

Alaimo, K., Olson, C. M., & Frongillo, E. A., Jr. (2001). Food insufficiency and American school-aged children's cognitive, academic and psychosocial development. *Pediatrics, 108*(1), 44–53.

Amen, D. (Producer/Director). (2004). *Which brain do you want?* [DVD]. Newport Beach, CA: Mindworks Press.

Baddeley, A. (1999). *Essentials of human memory.* East Sussex, UK: Psychology Press.

Barlow, J. (2003). *Study is first to confirm link between exercise and changes in brain.* Retrieved November 3, 2005, from News Bureau University of Illinois Champaign-Urbana Web site: http://www.news.uiuc.edu/scitips/03/0127exercise.html

Benton, D., & Cook, R. (1991). Vitamin and mineral supplements improve the intelligence scores and concentration of six year old children. *Personality and Individual Differences, 12*(11), 1151–1158.

Bloom, F., Beal, M., & Kupfer, D. (Eds.). (2003). *The Dana guide to brain health.* New York: Dana Press.

Bourtchouladze, R. (2002). *Memories are made of this.* London: Columbia University Press.

Burmark, L. (2002). *Visual literacy: Learn to see, see to learn.* Alexandria, VA: ASCD.

Buzan, T. (2003). *Mind maps for kids.* New York: HarperCollins.

Carper, J. (2000). *Your miracle brain.* New York: HarperCollins.

Carskadon, M. (1999). When worlds collide: Adolescent need for sleep versus societal demands. In K. Wahlstrom (Ed.), *Adolescent sleep needs and school starting times.* Bloomington, IN: Phi Delta Kappa Educational Foundation.

Children's Hospital Medical Center of Cincinnati. (2001). *Playground injuries more severe than motor vehicle crashes.* Retrieved October 1, 2005, from http://www.birf.info/prevent/prev-articles/prev-playground.html

Conyers, M., & Wilson, D. (2001). *Brainsmart nutrition: 10 foods that may support a healthy brain-body system.* Retrieved September 3, 2005, from http://www.brainsmart.com/10foods.asp

Damasio, A. (1999). *The feeling of what happens.* New York: Harcourt Brace.

DeFina, P. (2003). *The neurobiology of memory: Understand, apply, and assess student memory.* Paper presented at the Learning and the Brain Conference, Cambridge, MA.

Dennison, P., & Dennison, G. (1994). *Brain gym.* Ventura, CA: Edu-Kinesthetics.

Diamond, M. (2002). *Children and enrichment in action from Cambodia to California.* Paper presented at the Learning and the Brain Conference, Cambridge, MA.

Doran, S. M., Van Dongen, H. P. A., & Dinges, D. F. (2001). Sustained attention performance during sleep deprivation: Evidence of state instability. *Arch Italiennes de Biologie: Neurosc, 139,* 253–267.

Fallone, G., Acebo, C., Seifer, R., & Carskadon, M. A. (2005). Experimental restriction of sleep opportunity in children: Effects on teacher ratings. *Sleep, 28,* 1561–1567.

Feinstein, S. (2004). *Secrets of the teenage brain.* Thousand Oaks, CA: Corwin Press.

Friedland, R. P., Fritsch, T., Smyth, K. A., Koss, E., Lerner, A. J., Chen, C. H., et al. (2001, March 13). Patients with Alzheimer's disease have reduced activities in midlife compared with healthy control-group members. *Proceedings of the National Academy of Sciences, 98,* 3440.

Gamon, D., & Bragdon, A. (2001). *Learn faster and remember more.* New York: Barnes & Noble.

Gazzaniga, M. (1998). *The mind's past.* Berkeley: University of California Press.

Glasgow, N., & Hicks, C. (2003). *What successful teachers do.* Thousand Oaks, CA: Corwin Press.

Goldman, R., Klatz, R., & Berger, L. (1999). *Brain fitness.* New York: Doubleday.

Gordon, B., & Berger, L. (2003). *Intelligent memory.* New York: Viking Press.

Haddock, V. (2001). Tips for a better memory. *WebMd.* Retrieved January 18, 2006, from http://my.webmd.com/content/article/11/1674_51094.htm

Hagwood, S. (2006). *Memory power.* New York: Free Press.

Harvard Medical School. (n.d.). Head injury in children. *Aetna InteliHealth.* Retrieved May 19, 2005, from http://www.intelihealth.com/

Johnston, L. D., O'Malley, P. M., & Bachman, J. G. (2003). *Monitoring the future national survey: Results on drug use, 1975–2002. Volume I: Secondary school students* (NIH Publication No. 03–5375). Bethesda, MD: National Institute on Drug Abuse.

Kenyon, G. (2002). Mind mapping can help dyslexics. *BBC News.* Retrieved November 7, 2005, from http://news.bbc.co.uk/1/hi/education/1926739.stm

LeDoux, J. (2002). *Synaptic self.* New York: Viking.

Liotta, F. (2004). *Helmets are a necessity, not a fashion accessory* (Reprinted from *Blethen Maine Newspapers,* 2004). Retrieved October 18, 2005, from http://www.birf.info/prevent/prev-articles/prev-ski.html

Marzano, R., Pickering, D., & Pollack, J. (2001). *Classroom instruction that works.* Alexandria, VA: ASCD.

McEwen, B., & Lasley, E. (2002). *The end of stress as we know it.* Washington, DC: Joseph Henry Press.

McKhann, G., & Albert, M. (2002). *Keep your brain young.* New York: John Wiley & Sons.

Mednick, S. C., Nakayama, K., Cantero, J. L., Atienza, M., Levin, A. A., Pathak, N., et al. (2002). The restorative effect of naps on perceptual deterioration. *Nature Neuroscience, 5,* 677–681.

Nader, K. (2003, October 9). Re-coding human memories. *Nature, 425,* 71–72.

National Sleep Foundation. (n.d.). *Bring out the stars* [Quiz]. Retrieved November 22, 2005, from http://www.sleepforkids.org/html/stars2.html

Ngo, T., & Bhadkamkar, N. (1998). The cocktail party effect. *New Scientist, 2159,* 51–52.

Palinscar, A. S., & Brown, A. L. (1985). Reciprocal teaching: Activities to promote read(ing) with your mind. In T. L. Harris & E. J. Cooper (Eds.), *Reading, thinking and concept development: Strategies for the classroom.* New York: College Board.

Quartz, S., & Sejnowski, T. (2002). *Liars, lovers, and heroes: What the new brain science reveals about how we become who we are.* New York: HarperCollins.

Ratey, J. (2001). *A user's guide to the brain.* New York: Pantheon Books.

Roizen, M., & Oz, M. (2005). *You—the owner's manual: An insider's guide to the body that will make you healthier and younger.* New York: HarperCollins.

Sapolsky, R. M. (2004). *Why zebras don't get ulcers: The acclaimed guide to stress, stress-related diseases, and coping* (3rd ed.). New York: W. H. Freeman.

Schacter, D. L. (2002). *The seven sins of memory: How the mind forgets and remembers.* New York: Houghton Mifflin.

Schenk, J. (2000). *Learning, teaching and the brain.* Thermopolis, WY: Knowa.

Sifft, J., & Khalsa, G. (1991). Effect of educational kinesiology upon simple response times and choice response times. *Perceptual and Motor Skills, 73,* 1011–1015.

Small, G. (2002). *The memory bible.* New York: Hyperion.

Snowdon, D. (2001). *Aging with grace: What the nun study teaches us about leading longer, healthier, and more meaningful lives.* New York: Bantam Books.

Sprenger, M. (1999). *Learning and memory: The brain in action.* Alexandria, VA: ASCD.

Sprenger, M. (2003). *Differentiation through learning styles and memory.* Thousand Oaks, CA: Corwin Press.

Sprenger, M. (2005). *How to teach so students remember.* Alexandria, VA: ASCD.

Stickgold, R., Whidbee, D., Schirmer, B., Patel, V., & Hobson, J. (2000). Visual discrimination task improvement: A multi-step process occurring during sleep. *Journal of Cognitive Neuroscience, 12*(2).

Taylor, S. E., Klein, L. C., Lewis, B. P., Gruenewald, T. L., Gurung, R. A., & Updegraff, J. A. (2000). Biobehavioral responses to stress in females: Tend-and-befriend, not fight-or-flight. *Psychological Review, 107,* 411–429.

Walford, R. (2000). *Beyond the 120 year diet: How to double your vital years.* New York: Four Walls Eight Windows.

INDEX

**CORWIN
PRESS**

The Corwin Press logo—a raven striding across an open book—represents the union of courage and learning. Corwin Press is committed to improving education for all learners by publishing books and other professional development resources for those serving the field of PreK–12 education. By providing practical, hands-on materials, Corwin Press continues to carry out the promise of its motto: **"Helping Educators Do Their Work Better."**